How Firm a Foundation

The 400-Year History of Hampton Virginia's
St. John's Episcopal Church
The Oldest Anglican Parish in the Americas

James Tormey

Contents

Foreword

St. John's Episcopal Church in Hampton, Virginia, is the oldest Anglican parish in continuous existence in the Americas. Since its founding in 1610 it has occupied four buildings, each at a different site within the boundaries of present day Hampton. None of the four locations was far from the Hampton River where a small port grew that became the primary focus of Hampton during its first century and a half. The picturesque waterway, which like the town was originally called Southhampton, continues to be the scene of maritime activity, both commercial and recreational.

There have been other changes in the names of geographic features over the past four centuries. Shortly after its founding, the leaders of the community decided to change its name from Kecoughtan, the original Indian village, to Elizabeth City. Moreover, the name Elizabeth City applied to the entire county. The Indian name stuck, however, and the early inhabitants simply continued to call the settlement Kecoughtan at least until it became the town of Hampton late in the 17th century. I have therefore referred to the first and second churches as being located at Kecoughtan and use the designation Elizabeth City when referring to the county wide boundaries of the parish. With the passage of time, other name changes have evolved. At some time after the Revolution, for example, Point Comfort came to be called Old Point Comfort. Then in 1962, the City of Hampton annexed the entire area of Elizabeth City

County so that many communities, including the town of Phoebus, became part of Hampton.

The third church was built on property known as "Westwood's Town Quarter". The land was later bought by John Jones and became a part of his "Pembroke Plantation". Hence the reference to the third building as the Pembroke Church. There is a marker in St. John's Church today memorializing the five generations of the Jones family who worshipped at St. John's.

The fourth church at Hampton, built in 1728, is the present day church.

A reader may conclude that the church's history could be called the history of the town, particularly in the colonial period. This is due, in part, to the loss of church records during the Civil War, so that much of the records that survive are court records. Moreover, when it was the only church and performed functions such as care of the poor, the history of church and town closely paralleled each other.

Despite changes in name, and many turbulent events, particularly in the 19th century, the body of believers who worshipped here persevered. A person attending St. John's Church today would find much that was familiar if he could step back in time to the services of an earlier day. These are services that have brought comfort and spiritual sustenance to generations of worshippers.

To say that St. John's Church was "the church" in Hampton may sound presumptuous. In fact, however, it was the only church until 1699 when the colonial legislature acted to permit alternative denominations to exist. Moreover, support of the Anglican Church by the state continued until the American Revolution. With the advent of religious toleration and freedom other churches were established and grew until they achieved the prominent role they have today in the religious life of the community.

Locations of St. John's Church
Hampton, Virginia

1667

1624

1728

1610

Hampton Roads

Drawings by Shannon McCall

1/2 mile   1/4 mile   0   1/2 mile

Part I

The Colonial Period
1610 - 1783

One

A Place Called Kecoughtan

The Virginia Company of London sent three ships to America in December, 1606 on what was a momentous undertaking for the passengers, the company, and England. The men aboard the *Susan Constant, Godspeed,* and *Discovery* were to establish a colony primarily for commercial purposes, although the charter provided them by King James I also desired that the colonists spread Protestant Christianity in America.[1] The English were well aware that both the French and the Spanish were ahead of them in acquiring territories in the new world and intended to occupy the region between the French in the north and the Spanish to the south. Here the colonists expected to find riches and spread the Protestant religion as embodied by the Church of England.

The voyage across the Atlantic had a dismal beginning; the tiny fleet was restrained by bad weather off the coast of England. For six weeks, the ships rolled and pitched against howling headwinds. The passengers were miserable, including the Reverend Robert Hunt who had been appointed chaplain to the new colony. Hunt was violently ill and must have longed for the firm ground of Old Heathfield in southeast England, not far from the coast, where he had served as minister before opting for a new life in Virginia. We have the testimony of Captain John Smith that "Master Hunt, our preacher, was so sick that few expected his recovery."[2]

Captain Christopher Newport finally brought the *Susan Constant, Godspeed,* and *Discovery* into Chesapeake Bay and on April 29, 1607, the

3

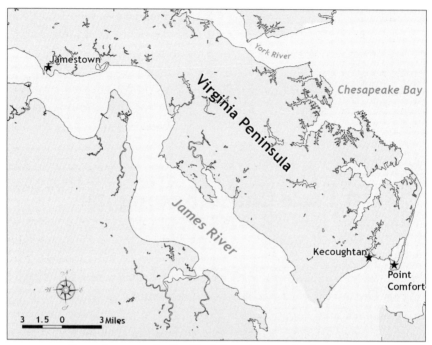

Kecoughtan was the first English settlement after Jamestown.

colonists set up a cross on Cape Henry where Robert Hunt led them in a service of thanksgiving. On the following day they reached Point Comfort where they saw Indians along the shore. Captain Newport called for the launching of the shallop, a flat-bottomed boat that enabled them to navigate shallow waters. Looking from the shore where they had been gathering strawberries, the Indians saw Newport with his hand over his heart, a sign of peace. The Indians then swam out to the boat and welcomed the English ashore near their village of Kecoughtan. Here the English feasted on strawberries, oysters, and bread. After eating they were entertained by dancing.[3]

The English rested for a few days at Kecoughtan before sailing up the James River to the site of Jamestown. Their orders from the Virginia Company directed them to locate upstream where they would presumably be safer from Spanish attack. Unfortunately, Jamestown was swampy and had no springs of fresh water. They could hardly have chosen an unhealthier place.

The unhealthy conditions did not cause the colonists to neglect religious services. John Smith wrote that these services were first held under an old sail for protection from the sun. There was a pulpit consisting of a bar of wood nailed to two trees. They later constructed a barn like building for a church with wood and earth walls similar to the houses in which they lived. They held morning and evening prayer each day. There were two sermons on Sunday and communion every three months. The Virginia Company's expectation from the beginning was that the colony would depend upon the grace of God for its success. Well-qualified men like Hunt were chosen as ministers and the people were expected to be aware of the need for God's help. Unfortunately, Robert Hunt died in 1608.

By contrast to the bleak outlook for the colonists at Christmas of 1607 in Jamestown, John Smith records his Christmas spent with the Indians at Kecoughtan in 1608 as a convivial time. Winter winds had driven Smith and a small party of men ashore as they were attempting to sail to Werowocomoco, the residence of Chief Powhatan.

"The next night being lodged at Kecoughtan, six or seven days the extreme wind, rain frost, and snow caused us to keep Christmas among the savages, where we were never more merry, nor fed on more plenty of good oysters, fish, flesh, wildfowl, and good bread, nor never had better fires in England than in the dry, warm, smoky houses of Kecoughtan."[4]

Captain George Percy, who replaced Smith as the leader of the colony, established Fort Algernon at Point Comfort in 1609, even as the colony was on the verge of failure. The timely arrival of Lord De La Warr in 1610 enabled the colony to continue because he brought needed supplies and more settlers. Sir Thomas Gates was en route to Fort Algernon from Jamestown on July 6, 1610 when a longboat from the the fort was lost and driven away by wind and current. Henry Blunt, an Englishman, while attempting to recover the boat, was murdered by Indians. In reprisal, on July 9, 1610 Gates attacked the village of Kecoughtan where Pochins, the son of Powhatan, was the chief.[5] The Indians of Kecoughtan were subservient to Powhatan, the paramount chief of the Algonquian Indians in tidewater Virginia. Chief Powhatan had previously conquered Kecoughtan in 1596/1597 and dispersed the surviving Kecoughtan Indians whom he replaced with people loyal to him.[6]. But the name Kecoughtan continued to be used by the Indians. It means "inhabitants of a great town" which was appropriate for a place that had been home for a thousand people.[7]

What a sad irony that the very Indians who had welcomed the English in 1607, and John Smith at Christmas in 1608, were driven from their homes and replaced by the people to whom they had shown hospitality. Notwithstanding the earlier welcome by the Indians, Sir Thomas Gates chose to seize a place that seemed valuable to the English. Kecoughtan was a logical location to establish a settlement. It helped to secure the peninsula where the James River met Chesapeake Bay. It had springs of fresh water, abundant seafood nearby, and was healthier than the swampy land at Jamestown. There were fields already planted and more that had been cleared by earlier occupants of the town of Kecoughtan.

July 9, 1610, the date on which the English took possession of Kecoughtan, marked the beginning of what is now known as the City of Hampton. Because the English installed a minister here it was also the beginning of the new Anglican parish. The Reverend William Mays, who was the first minister, was sent from Jamestown to serve the people at the new settlement.

Two

The First Church, 1610

Drawing by Shannon McCall.

The exact location of the English settlement in Kecoughtan in 1610 is not known. It probably was near the mouth of a small stream named Church Creek near an area today known as Merrimac Shores. Indian habitations were most likely to have been located along the shores that were well drained for agriculture and easily accessible to fishing grounds.

Reading from top and left to right: fish bone, bone ball, hatchet tomahawk, arrow heads, locally made pipes, and pipe stems.

Indian and English artifacts from the Brittingham excavations near the site of the first church at Kecoughtan.

Archeological evidence from both the Indian and English occupants has been found in the area.[1]

Whether there was a separate building devoted to a church or the services were held in a home is likewise unknown. Considering the daily frequency of morning and evening prayer and the assignment of the Rev. William Mays as minister it is probable that there was some specific space dedicated to religious services. That location is referred to as the "first site" of the church at Kecoughtan.

Days must have seemed long to the Reverend Mays and the members of his small congregation. In addition to trying to find food while on the alert for Indian attacks, the men had to build defenses as well as houses in which to live. In 1611, an Englishman named William Parker was captured by Indians near the settlement. Lord De La Warr's actions to meet the need for defenses were mentioned in a contemporary report by Captain George Percy:

"My lord general about this time sent Captain Howldcrofte to build
a fort in the woods near Kecoughtan. The which, being finished, my
lord named the same "Charles Fort..."[2]

The English built a second fort, this one named for Prince Henry.
Forts Charles and Henry stood on opposite sides of a small river, at first
called the Southampton River, which flowed into the James. The settlers
eventually changed the name to the Hampton River.

The arrival of Sir Thomas Dale with three hundred settlers in May,
1611 brought another military leader to Virginia who was to have an
important impact on the colony. Rather than proceeding immediately
to Jamestown, he put men to work improving the defenses of the two
small forts at Kecoughtan. He also had more crops planted in the fields
near the settlement. Thomas Dale reported to the Council of the Virginia
Company:

"...we on all hands fell to digging and cleaning the ground and
setting of corn, and in four or five days we had set more ground
about Fort Henry than Sir Thomas Gates found set by the Indians in the
year before."

Thomas Dale left some of his men to continue the work at Kecoughtan,
with instructions that he was to receive weekly reports on their progress.[3]

Thomas Dale brought to all his activities the same zeal he had
demonstrated at Kecoughtan. In particular, he was zealous in imposing
discipline through martial law; with a wide range of punishments to be
imposed on lawbreakers. He did not neglect the "laws divine" with a
similar range of harsh sanctions. All persons within the colony had to
present themselves to the minister who would make a determination on
the sufficiency of his or her faith. Those found deficient would be required
to attend instruction on Sunday afternoon. The disobedient were punished
by whipping.[4]

A minister of remarkable intelligence and high qualifications named
Alexander Whitaker accompanied Thomas Dale to the Virginia colony.
There were now three ministers in the colony: William Bucke at Jamestown,
William Mays at Kecoughtan, and Whitaker, who accompanied Thomas

Dale when he established the settlement at Henrico a few months later. Although all three ministers were of the Church of England, they were influenced by Calvinist theology. Alexander Whitaker was motivated by a calling to bring Christianity to the Indians whom he credited as having "reasonable souls and intellectual facilities as well as us."[5]

The colonists were making progress in producing food under healthier conditions and a cash crop economy involving tobacco was soon to develop. By 1613, John Rolfe had developed a milder tobacco that could be used by the settlers and even shipped to England for sale in a market previously dominated by Spanish produced tobacco. Tobacco would take the place of gold and precious minerals that were never found as the economic justification of the Virginia colony. Relations with the Indians were not improving, however, as the natives resisted the continuing English encroachment on their territory.

The marriage of Pocahontas to John Rolfe in 1614 began a period of peace that lasted for nearly eight years. Pocahontas had befriended the colonists at Jamestown in 1607 and 1608 when she was a young girl and had pleaded for the life of John Smith when he was captured by Powhatan. A cessation of hostilities was welcome to both the English and the Indians. Powhatan released the Englishman, William Parker, who had been captured at Kecoughtan three years earlier. The English did not recognize Parker at first for he appeared in complexion and dress to be an Indian. But he joyfully identified himself by his ability to speak English.[6]

Additional settlements, such as Shirley Hundred, were established along the James River but the population was sparse, primarily because so many colonists grew sick and died. In 1616, John Rolfe stated in a report prepared for King James that the whole population of the colony was 351 persons, of which 59 were women and children - "a small number to advance so great a work." At Kecoughtan, Rolfe reported "are 20, whereof 11 are farmers ... Captain George Webb, commander; Mr. William Mays minister there."[7]

The Virginia Company designated Kecoughtan as one of the four "boroughs" (later "corporations") of Virginia; the others being James City, Charles City and Henricus. The boroughs included the settlement and its surrounding territory. Plantations, consisting of one hundred or more persons, were also to have political status. In 1619, seven recognized plantations in addition to the four boroughs each sent two elected representatives to the first meeting of the General Assembly.[8] The borough of Kecoughtan elected Captain William Tucker and William Capps to be its representatives. They asked the General Assembly to change the name of Kecoughtan to Elizabeth City.

William Mays, the first minister at Kecoughtan, ended his ministry there in 1620 after ten years of service. Mays later returned to England. He was replaced by George Keith who came to Virginia in 1617.[9] In compensation for his employment, a minister could expect a salary, usually paid in tobacco or corn by the members of the congregation, a home to live in, and one hundred acres of glebe land to which the Virginia Company would assign tenants. One half the produce of the land went to the tenants with the remainder to the minister.

The Virginia Company and the newly formed General Assembly exercised authority over the church as there were no bishops in Virginia. Among other measures such as requiring church attendance, they prescribed parish boundaries. These boundaries were the same as the corresponding civil boundaries. Therefore, when the Borough of Kecoughtan was renamed the Borough of Elizabeth City in 1620, the entire area within the Borough of Elizabeth City was within the Parish of Elizabeth City.

*Detail from window showing the baptism of Pocahontas. The marriage of
Pocahontas to John Rolfe was followed by a cessation of hostilities.*

Three

A Place of Refuge

The Virginia settlers continued to use the name Kecoughtan for many years and to this day it lives on in names of places and institutions in Hampton, Many persons have lamented the change of name from Kecoughtan to Elizabeth City because of the beauty of the Indian name. It is not possible to say how much of the desire to change the name was due to the desire to avoid an Indian name and how much to please King James whose daughter Elizabeth was to be honored by the name Elizabeth City. It is impossible to know how many settlers continued to use the name Kecoughtan or when they began to use the name Hampton for the settlement near the Hampton River.

The Reverend George Keith, who had followed Reverend William Mays at Elizabeth City Parish, voluntarily removed himself from that position and became minister at Martin's Hundred.[1] The hundreds were large plantations having the need to form a parish and the ability to support it. Martin's Hundred was formed in 1617 and Smith's Hundred in 1618. More land was brought under cultivation as the process of founding hundreds continued.[2]

Mrs. Mary Robinson of the Parish of St. Olave in London bequeathed two hundred pounds for the poor people of Virginia in 1618. This money and other contributions were used for building a church at Smith's Hundred and providing communion silver.[3] This silver would eventually come to Elizabeth City Parish.

The Reverend Thomas White succeeded the Reverend George Keith as the minister of Elizabeth City Parish in 1622. He was sent by the Virginia Company in London and described as "a man of good sufficiency for learning, and recommended for integrity & uprightness of life."[4]

Mortality continued to be high, particularly among the new arrivals in Virginia. In the year following March, 1620, approximately one thousand persons had died either in route to or in Virginia. An estimated four fifths of these were newcomers.[5] Even though it was a period of peace, the combination of disease, malnutrition, and exhausting work took a heavy toll. In an effort to improve the health of newcomers after the strain of the Atlantic passage, a guest house, or hospital, was built at Kecoughtan capable of accommodating fifty persons.[6]

In November 1620, the Virginia Company awarded land in Elizabeth City Corporation to Mr. Daniel Gookin in return for the transport of forty young cattle and fifty men along with thirty other passengers. Gookin came from Newce's Town in Ireland along with Thomas and William Newce. Gookin joined the Newce brothers at the place they called "New Porte Newce." and kept up the plantation after they died.[7] It may surprise the reader that the boundary of Elizabeth City Corporation extended some twelve miles west from Chesapeake Bay and also that it extended into the south side of Hampton Roads.

Most of the English believed there was no longer danger of attack from the Indians. Powhatan had died in 1618 and the leadership of the tribes had passed to his brothers. Opechancanough, who was the real leader among the brothers, continued to profess friendship to the succession of English governors. We do not know when Opechancanough decided to orchestrate an uprising, involving tribes that he could control, that might destroy the English. He probably concluded that the English, whom he resented deeply, had to be attacked when he realized that their numbers were continuing to increase. He could not help but notice the increasing number of ships that were bringing more settlers to the colony. When the earlier hostilities had ended in 1614 the English tended to spread out in small settlements rather than live in towns. English investors founded a number of plantations whose work force was drawn from the ranks of the indentured who were lured to Virginia by the promise of eventual land ownership. Living in small settlements and plantations made the settlers more vulnerable to attack.

On the morning of Good Friday, March 22, 1622, Opechancanough's men who had enjoyed good relations with the English in the James River Valley came to homes and farms where they had been accustomed to being welcomed. Once there, they seized whatever tools or weapons that were on hand and attacked the surprised settlers. When their resistance was overcome, buildings and crops were burned. The Uprising of 1622 extended along the entire length of James River settlements with the exception of the vicinity of Jamestown and Kecoughtan. Jamestown had been alerted and drove off attackers; Kecoughtan was probably spared because of its strong defenses. At a time when English families were on friendly terms with visiting Indians, it was a devastating attack in which 347 settlers died, over one-quarter of the population. Among those killed was the Reverend Keith, formerly minister at Elizabeth City, who was minister at Martin's Hundred at the time of the uprising.[8]

A severe blow was dealt to English hopes of bringing Christianity to the Indians. The Company had empowered Mr. George Thorpe, a deeply religious man, to build a college near Henrico where Indians might live while their children were educated. Thorpe was killed and the buildings were destroyed. The Great Massacre of 1622 ended hopes for educating Indians at Henrico College which was never rebuilt.

In the confusion that followed the uprising, the Governor issued instructions for the settlers to fall back to Jamestown, Shirley, Elizabeth City Corporation and a few other plantations that could be strongly defended. All others were to be abandoned. The effect on Elizabeth City was a sudden increase in population. There were 358 people listed in the muster of persons in Elizabeth City Corporation in February 1623.[9]

Among the survivors fleeing to Kecoughtan were Edward Waters and his wife. They had been captured by Nansemond Indians south of the James River but had managed to escape and cross the river.[10] John and Anne Laydon brought their family as refugees to live in Elizabeth City and would have worshipped at the church at Kecoughtan. John Laydon had come with the first settlers in 1607 and was shown on the passenger list of the *Susan Constant* as a laborer. His wife Anne came as a fourteen year old servant of Mistress Forrest in 1608. Theirs was the first marriage in Virginia and their daughter, Virginia, was the first child born to the English here. There is a memorial to Virginia Laydon at St. John's Church.

1622 was a poor year for crops in Virginia as much land was abandoned after the uprising. The output from several industries such as wine making and silk production had not proven successful. French wine makers had not been able to produce a satisfactory wine from the grapes grown in Elizabeth City and the return from making silk was not worth the labor required. Vigilance was necessary in the face of sporadic Indians attacks during the summer, particularly at the Gookin plantation in Elizabeth City.

The effects of the uprising were long lasting. Resentment felt by the Indian people toward the English who had appropriated their land was now matched by survivors' resentment towards the Indians whom they saw as their enemy. William Capps of Hampton, whose land included the "Little England" plantation in Elizabeth City, expressed the view of many:

> "God forgive me I think the last massacre killed all our Countrie, besides them they killed, they burst the heart of all the rest."[11]

Four

The Second Church

Drawing by Shannon McCall.

The decision was made in 1623 to build a church at what has come to be known as the second site of St. John's Church. It was located on the east side of the Hampton River in a more central location for the settlers. Because of its situation near the Hampton River it was more accessible by boat. Close by the second church was a spring of clear, sweet water.

Archeological explorations recorded by Eleanor S. Holt determined that the second church at Kecoughtan was a wooden frame structure resting on a stone foundation with outer dimensions of about 23 by 52 feet. There was a small adjoining eight by nine foot foundation which supported a covered entryway. The foundation consisted of bricks and cobblestone from local sources. Tile flooring was found at either end of the church and along an aisle about six feet wide. The tiles, like the brick, were hand made locally and were laid without mortar. In later years, the settlers buried some of their prominent citizens within the church. The remains of three gravestones have been found but many more were buried there over the years.[1]

By the time of construction of the second church in 1624, the Governor and Council had established that master carpenters and bricklayers were paid four shillings per day.

If the local residents furnished the materials for construction, Captain Tucker, the local commander, could have paid the workmen for construction of the church using funds collected by the church wardens.[2] Edward Waters, who had fled to Kecoughtan in 1622 was one of the two church wardens.

In the early years of the Virginia colony, the minister of a church appointed two laymen from his congregation to be church wardens. They were leading citizens of the community; and, in the case of Edward Waters, one who had survived the hazards of colonial life. Waters was a passenger on the *Seaventure,* shipwrecked on Bermuda in 1609 on its way to Virginia. He reached Virginia on the *Patience* which was built on Bermuda under the direction of Sir George Somers and then returned with Somers to Bermuda. Edward Waters was one of three men left on Bermuda to maintain the claim of the British on the islands and gained a position of prominence as member of the council. He came to Virginia in 1618 or 1619 where he married Grace O'Niel. As mentioned earlier, the Nansemond Indians captured Edward and Grace Waters during the Uprising of 1622. After escaping to Kecoughtan they settled there and he later became a member of the House of Burgesses as well as a warden of the church at Kecoughtan.[3]

Construction of a new church suggests that, though discouraged by losses from Indian attacks and sickness, the settlers had the determination

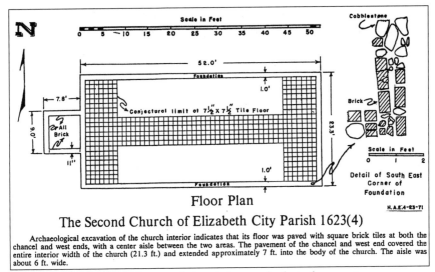

Floor Plan of the second church from archeological excavations.

to make a success of the colony. Tobacco was the economic salvation of Virginia; it not only brought returns in the English market but also was a medium of exchange in Virginia. The salary of ministers was payable in tobacco as were fines for failure to attend church. Planters who succeeded in producing a tobacco crop could easily establish credit for purchases of products from England. Elizabeth City planters near the James River or the Hampton River were well-situated to ship tobacco to England and receive manufactured goods in return. Jamestown and Kecoughtan were beginning to emerge as communities. Even though with mainly wooden structures and few amenities, there were prospects of growth and economic health.

Whether or not the Reverend Thomas White survived to see the second church is not known. A report of the General Assembly dated October 10, 1624 stated that Mr. White being dead, Governor Sir Francis Wyatt appointed the Reverend Jonas Stockton to be minister at Elizabeth City Parish.[4]

The Reverend Stockton was considered a highly effective minister. His influence extended beyond religious matters since after August, 1626 he served as one of the justices of the Elizabeth City court that was held monthly. He warned the settlers of Indian treachery and was of

St. John's communion silver, made in London in 1618.

the opinion that conversion of the Indians would not occur until all the Indian priests had been killed.[5] The Reverend Reverdy Estill, writing in 1907, attributes that opinion to panic following the uprising of 1622 for otherwise Stockton was reputed to be a godly and humane man.

The Reverend Stockton must have been a busy minister; there were the newly arrived to meet and funeral rites for the dead. The names of twenty-seven settlers appear on a list of burials in Elizabeth City Corporation in 1624 (and this must have been only a partial list). A more pleasant duty would have been the baptism of Margaret, the daughter of John and Anne Laydon. She was the fourth daughter of the Laydons, all of whom were listed as "born in Virginia". The Laydon family had to move in the wake of the Uprising of 1622 to Hampton, a place where his family would be safe while he continued to earn his living as a farmer.

The second church was a gathering place for the settlers before and after services. The many pipe fragments found on the site show that the early Virginians were consumers as well as producers of tobacco. They used pipes made in Virginia as well as those from England. Virginia made pipes can be distinguished by the red or brown clay from which they were manufactured. Archeologists have dated the pipes from the diameter of the stemholes which grew smaller as the style of pipes changed over time.

Among the many personal items found was a thimble at the gravesite of a woman. It was probably brought by her from England and remained one of her prized possessions for the rest of her life. The ability of a woman to make clothes for herself and her family was invaluable in colonial days and a thimble was essential to the seamstress.

Early in the life of the second church, it became the second congregation to benefit from the gift of communion silver made by Mrs. Mary Robinson and donors in England. The silver, made in 1618, went first to the church at Smith's Hundred which was destroyed in the Massacre of 1622. The silver was entrusted to Sir George Yeardley who died in 1627. His widow, Temperance Yeardley delivered the silver to the Court at James City which ordered Mr. William Claiborne to inventory the goods at Smith's Hundred. It is believed that Claiborne gave the silver to Captain William Tucker to be delivered to the church at Kecoughtan.[6]

Since then, the silver has been in continuous use from 1628 at the second church, at the third church, and now at St. John's Church in Hampton. It has been in use longer than any other English communion silver in America.

The second church must have seemed not only a place of worship for the people of Kecoughtan but also a tie to their mother country. At the church they could hear the reassuring words of the *Book of Common Prayer* of 1559, just as they would in England:

> "Glory be to the father, and to the sonne, and to the holy
> ghoste. As it was in the beginninge, is nowe, and ever shall be;
> worlde without ende. Amen.
> Praise ye the Lorde"

How the church at the second site may have appeared.

Five

Church and the Colonial Government

Credit should go to Sir Edwin Sandys, a prominent leader of the Virginia Company of London, for the impact he had on religious life in Virginia. Sandys had liberal views that were a cause of friction with King James I. It was Sandys' view that the colonists should enjoy self-government that reached fruition in the creation of a General Assembly with elected representatives as well as a church without ecclesiastic courts. Sandys also selected ministers for the colony who were influenced by Calvinist views but who sought to reform the church from within.[1] There was no doubt of the importance of the role of the church. In the absence of a bishop, the Governor or the General Assembly performed some of the functions performed in England by a bishop such as the granting of marriage licenses and the appointing of ministers.[2] Among the first laws enacted by the General Assembly in 1623 were the following:

> " That there shall be in every plantation, where the people use to meet for the worship of God, a house or roome sequestered for that purpose, and not to be for any temporal use whatsoever, and a place empaled in, sequestered only for the burial of the dead.
>
> That whosoever shall absent himself from divine service any Sunday without an excuse shall forfeit a pound of tobacco, and he that absenteth himself a month shall forfeit 50lb. Of tobacco.

That no minister be absent from his church above two months in all the yeare upon penalty of forfeiting halfe his means, and whosoever shall absent himself above fawre months in the year shall forfeit his whole means and cure.

That no man dispose of any of his tobacco before the minister be satisfied, upon pain of forfeiture double his part of the minister's means, and one man of every plantation to collect his means out of the first and best tobacco and corn."[3]

The leaders of Virginia left no doubt that there were to be places for public worship, that the people would attend services, that ministers would not absent themselves overmuch and that they would be justly compensated.

Despite the power of government officials in the person of the commanders of towns, their power was far from absolute. This was demonstrated in the controversy that arose between Captain William Tucker, the Commander at Elizabeth City, and the Reverend Rowland Graeme, who in 1628 succeeded Jonas Stockton as minister of the second church. The following account is gleaned from court records. In April 1628 Captain Tucker sent a man to the Reverend Graeme demanding the use of the sails and mast of Mr. Graeme's boat. Mr. Graeme refused the demand saying, "If Captain Tucker have anything to say to me let him come here for I owe him not so much service as to go to him." A second visit and request met with denial when the Reverend Graeme said, "I am going to serve Communion and God must be served before the King." Then the men sent by Captain Tucker decided to seize the boat. When she overheard the men saying that they were going to take the boat, Mrs. Graeme called out to warn her husband. Running out of the house, the infuriated minister called to a servant for his gun and said, "I will shoot you if any man stir out of the path." Once again, Captain Tucker sent for the boat. This time he sent a warrant for its seizure. After reading the warrant, the Reverend Graeme said, "You shall have no boat here. My boat shall not go off my ground, (even) if the Governor send twenty warrants."[4] Unfortunately, The records of the court do not show how this matter was resolved, but it is assumed that the two men made up their differences because they continued to serve as commander and minister of Elizabeth City for several more years.

More details are known of the life of William Tucker than of the Reverend Rowland Graeme, his ministerial counterpart. Tucker had come to Virginia in 1610 with Lord De La Warr and in 1623 he married Mary Thompson who had just come over from England. Tucker's daughter Elizabeth was born in 1624. He had fourteen white servants, an Indian servant, and three African servants: Anthony, Isabell, and their son William, who presumably were baptized at the second church.[5]

The General Assembly continued to exercise influence over the church. In 1632 it decreed that ministers would choose their church wardens at Easter of each year. There was a court in Jamestown each June where ministers and church wardens would report offenders against the laws regarding religion. Marriages, baptisms and funerals held in each parish were also reported to the Jamestown Court.

When the price of tobacco fell in the London markets, the effective salary of the ministers decreased. The General Assembly sought to offset this by decreeing that the twentieth calf, pig, and goat produced on every farm should be given to the minister. The fee paid to the minister for a wedding was set at two shillings and for a funeral at one shilling. There was no fee for a baptism.

To meet the cost of building and repairing churches, the General Assembly directed that a group consisting of the local commissioners, minister, churchwardens, and leading citizens should determine the needs of the parish and then let contracts for the work. Payment would be made by assessments on the members of the parish. Assessments included provision for sick and indigent persons. This group of citizens within the parish was the predecessor of the vestry. The General Assembly in 1642 created the vestry system within the church and gave the vestries some of the duties previously performed by the minister. Significant in the legal code was the provision that the vestry had the power to select a minister who would be recommended to the governor for appointment. The vestry was also given the power to prefer charges against any minister on the grounds of misconduct. While the governor had the power to exact penalties for misconduct, the act of separating a minister from his position could only be accomplished by the General Assembly. These actions indicate how the church and government in Virginia adapted to the absence of bishops and ecclesiastical courts.[6]

Another link between church and state in early Virginia was the practice of "benefit of clergy." By this doctrine, a person guilty of a capital crime could, if it were the first offense, obtain remission of his penalty by presenting himself before a clergyman and demonstrating that he could read. To insure this only occurred once in the life of an offender, he was branded on the hand to show he had received benefit of clergy. In 1629, William Reade, then thirteen or fourteen years old, was accused of manslaughter after mortally wounding John Burrowes with his knife. He was tried before a jury at Kecoughtan and found guilty of manslaughter. When asked what he had to say for himself he responded that he did not wish to die and demanded the benefit of clergy. Subsequently he was turned over to The Reverend Graeme to determine whether or not he was literate.[7] The practice of benefit of clergy continued throughout the colonial period.

The influence that the colonial government had over the church in Virginia seems unreal to us today. Some of this influence evolved in the absence of bishops who would have given direction to the affairs of the church. On the local level, the church performed governmental functions, including providing for the poor, that continued until the American Revolution.

Six

17th Century Parish Life

The Elizabeth City Parish population continued to grow during the middle years of the 17th century. It was a time of growth for the entire Virginia Colony as the rewards of tobacco and land grants acted as incentives to immigration. Even though the government in England would have preferred towns and a more diversified economy, it was natural that the new colonists should seek farmland rather than settle in towns.

In 1634, the General Assembly reapportioned the Virginia Colony into eight counties. Elizabeth City County was affected, losing land to what eventually was to become Warwick and York Counties. In 1637, the land south of the James River was also separated from Elizabeth City County. Despite its small size, Elizabeth City was the most densely populated county and was to remain so for the remainder of the 17th century. Its population had grown by over five hundred persons in the ten years following the muster of 1624 even with the decrease in its boundaries. Kecoughtan, as it was still called by many, was a thriving settlement. It and Jamestown were the only settlements in the Virginia Colony close to being towns.[1]

As the population grew it was customary to create new parishes within the boundaries of existing ones. It is possible, but it has not been proven, there was another church in Elizabeth City County besides the one ministered to by Rowland Graeme.

In 1635, the Reverend William Wilkinson was appointed to be the minister at Elizabeth City Parish. He was a graduate of Oxford. It is known that at least three of his predecessors had attended either Oxford or Cambridge. He received a land patent in Lynhaven of seven hundred acres, one hundred of which was for bringing himself and his wife Naomi to Virginia.[2]

Gathering for church services was one of the few events in the life of colonist offering relief from the rigors of their daily life. It was the only regular event which included the entire family. Court days were for men only; they were often the time for much consumption of alcohol. Muster days, when the militia assembled, emphasized the role of men. Sundays, by contrast, were a time when neighbors could gather together before and after church to exchange news and maintain friendships. It was a time for unmarried men to meet the daughters or widows of parishioners. Public announcements were made. Parishioners arriving from a distance on horseback or in wagons were often invited to a meal at a friend's home nearer the church. If the minister were absent, a lay person would conduct the services. Prayers were read from the Book of Common Prayer and a homily was preached. Psalm singing was led by a reader since so many of the congregation could not read. These congregational customs afforded a respite from the struggle to establish homes in a new country.[3]

The need to defend themselves, however, was not forgotten. One of the artifacts recovered at the second church was the blade of a 17th century sword that bears the name of the maker, Andrea Ferara. This may have been one of 110 swords recorded in a 1624 inventory of weapons in Elizabeth City Corporation. It was probably worn to church in response to a decree of the General Assembly stating all who bore arms should bring them to Sunday services. Various musket parts found on the site attest to the fact that settlers complied with this regulation.[4]

Weddings were a less regular event in the life of the parish. During the seventeenth century men continued to outnumber women by a large majority. As a result, an unmarried woman emigrating from England could expect to find suitors in Virginia. Unless they so chose, few remained unmarried within three months after their arrival. A similar situation applied to widows except that a widow generally had control of the property left to her by her late husband. In order to exert control over their property, many widows entered into pre-nuptial agreements with

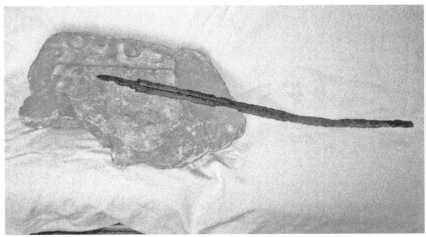

Fragment of tombstone and blade of 17th century sword found at site of the second church. Colonists who bore arms were required to bring them to church.

their second husbands. Even though a woman did not enjoy all the legal rights of a man at this time, the contribution and influence of a wife was critical to the success of a household or a plantation.

Weddings were performed at the Kecoughtan Church, with the clergyman administering the wedding vows. After the service, the men attending might fire their muskets to celebrate the event. Feasting and dancing followed as had been the custom in England. Because the colonists who lived on remote plantations desired to make the most of their limited opportunities to enjoy social events, wedding celebrations were less restrained than in England. If Indian attacks were threatened, guns were not fired in order to conserve ammunition.

Funerals were naturally more somber occasions than weddings but they were usually followed by firing of muskets, often as provided for in the will of the deceased. Since the persons attending were likely to have traveled some distance to be in attendance, the family of the deceased felt obliged to provide copious food and drink for their refreshment. The deceased, if he were of the same mind, could provide in his will for the quantities of refreshments to be made available to the guests at the funeral.[5]

Daniel Hopkinson, an English merchant on a trading voyage to Virginia on the ship *Tristram and Jane*, fell sick while here and wrote his

Ceramic bowl of rare German Weserware found at the site of the second church.

will in November, 1636. In the will, he directed his executor to arrange for his body to be interred in the church at Kecoughtan and the appropriate fees be paid for this privilege. The records of the *Tristram and Jane* show that fourteen gallons of white wine were consumed at his funeral. Presumably his funeral was attended by his shipmates and persons known from his trading voyage.[6]

For those who chose not to attend church services, there were penalties imposed by the court. In 1644, forty-six persons in Kecoughtan were required to pay fines in tobacco for non-attendance at church. As there are known to have been cock fights in neighboring counties, it is possible that attendance at the cock fights was the cause of their absence.[7]

Then as now, parents placed a high value on education. While some were able to teach their children at home, others would have needed outside help. Parents would have looked to the ministers of the church because they were learned men. Some of the ministers conducted schools for children in the parish. Other parents went so far as to send their children back to England for their education, but that would not have been feasible for most.

In 1635, Benjamin Syms made free schooling possible for the children of Elizabeth City by creating an endowment in his will. He left two hundred acres of land on the Back River and eight cattle for the support of a school teacher to operate a free school for the education of local children. In 1643, the General Assembly commended him for his "godly disposition and good intent – for the encouraging of all others in like pious performances." The school flourished at its schoolhouse constructed on the land where the herd of cattle increased.

Evidently Mr. Syms' example did encourage others because in 1659 a similar bequest for a free school was made by Dr. Thomas Eaton. By his will, an even larger endowment was created: five hundred acres of land, twelve cattle, two slaves, and some farm utensils. The school's location was near the head of the Back River. Administration of the estate was left to local officials including the church ministers and wardens in the county. The two schools or their successors continued and the financial legacy continues to exist today in the Hampton public school system.[8]

The vestry became the part of the congregation that was a continuing influence in the life of the parish. Ministers might come and go but the vestry remained. Vestrymen were leading citizens. While the church wardens appointed by the minister were expected to report offenders including drunkards to the courts, the vestry had additional, well-defined responsibilities. These included providing for the poor, sick, and aged. The vestry was also responsible for apprenticing orphans and illegitimate children to persons who would give them homes and teach them to read and write. Each vestry also was required to have neighbors confirm the boundaries of their adjoining lands every four years by a procedure known as "processing of their lands". The vestry's role in the life of the community extended well beyond matters of worship.[9]

Seven

Strife and the Great Storm

Conditions in the Virginia Colony were affected by the political climate that prevailed in England. The ascension of Charles II to the throne began a tumultuous period of unrest. King Charles, as had his father Charles I, attempted to impose the divine right of kings. The immediate effect on life in Virginia was the imposition of Sir John Harvey as Governor.

Sir John Harvey was arrogant, arbitrary, and rapacious. He shared King Charles' view that Virginia was the private property of the king. Naturally, he encountered resistance from the outset of his appointment in 1629. By 1635, Harvey had so offended the leaders of the colony that they had him arrested and sent back to England. Once in England, Harvey turned the tables on his accusers, convinced the king of his innocence, and was sent back to Virginia.

In January, 1637 Sir John Harvey read his commission to be governor again at the church at Kecoughtan. Selection of the church for this announcement indicates it was a focal point for the community. With a pardon from the king for all those who had taken part in his removal in 1635, Harvey used Kecoughtan as the capital for the colony. Virginia was subjected to three more years of Sir John Harvey's administration. By the end of that time the evidence of his misdeeds reached England and he was recalled in disgrace.[1]

Virginia was for the most part spared the unsettling actions of the

English Civil War when the Puritans rose up against the king. Very few persons in the colony were opposed to the king. Virginia did have some people of religious affiliations other than Anglican. Seeking to avoid the influence of the Anglican church, three hundred Puritans left Virginia in 1649 to go to Maryland.[2] Because he was a Puritan, the son of Daniel Gookin, who had established a plantation in Newport News, felt compelled to leave Virginia and went to live in Boston.[3]

Virginia steadfastly maintained its loyalty to the Crown for which it was later called "The Old Dominion". After the war there were loyalists who left England and chose to come to Virginia. Among these were some ministers from the Church of England who otherwise might not have elected to emigrate. These were men of good education and character who had little difficulty finding a parish to serve. With the passage of time this source of supply diminished and there grew to be a shortage of ministers in the colony which continued for many years. Elizabeth City Parish, however, did not seem to have difficulty in retaining a minister. Perhaps it offered a better living because of the relatively favorable population density. The Reverend Justinian Aylmer, a Cambridge graduate, became minister here in 1645 and retained the position until 1667.

There was also a Quaker presence in Virginia. In 1661, the Reverend Aylmer became involved with Mr. Thomas Bushrod, a Quaker, in a court case. Because Mrs. Bushrod had been invited to attend the Anglican Church, Mr. Bushrod angrily called Mr. Aylmer and another minister "a couple of Episcopal knaves" and "antichrists come from the Pope". Mr. Bushrod had cause to regret his abusive remarks because he was ordered to be held without bail until the next quarter court at James City.[4]

Like his predecessor, Mr. Wilkinson, the Reverend Aylmer patented a large holding of land. Mr. Wilkinson chose land at Lynhaven and Mr. Aylmer patented 495 acres on Mobjack Bay in Gloucester County.[5] These patents indicate that colonial ministers were men of sufficient means to acquire property. Under the indentured labor system of that period these two ministers were probably able to enjoy income from the land.

While the majority of parishioners worked on plantations, the community near the church would have included persons finding employment here at the developing port. There was a tobacco warehouse after 1633 where planters had to bring their tobacco for inspection as well as a number of ordinaries that had been established as early as the 1620s. These provided refreshment to persons attending court, to men from the sailing ships and to the local citizens. There was activity for the repair of ships and wagons. A ferry was in operation across the Hampton River. When William Claiborne began his trading business, he chose Elizabeth City as his base of operations.

William Claiborne was a man of extraordinary ability. Besides being Surveyor of the Colony, he was appointed to the Council four years after his arrival. After the Indian uprising in 1622, he fought in military expeditions against the Indians. As a reward for his services he received a patent for seven hundred fifty acres of land, including land on the banks of the Hampton River.[6] He built the first windmill in Elizabeth City at the mouth of the Hampton River.[7] He later sold some of this property to Captain William Jarvis who used it for a trading plantation. The Jarvis plantation subsequently became the land on which the town of Hampton was laid out. Although William Claiborne is chiefly remembered today for his land dispute with Maryland, he should also be remembered for recognizing the potential of Hampton as a seaport and acting upon it.

By 1667, the community at Elizabeth City appeared to have passed through the trials of the mid-1600s. Virginia had ridden out the misrule of Sir John Harvey as Governor under King Charles I. With the ascension of King Charles II, Virginia could take credit for having been loyal to the monarchy.

In 1644, despite his advanced age, Opechancanough had organized another uprising. Although by then in his nineties, the aged chief had not lost the ability to plan one last attack on his English enemies. He still had influence over the Mattaponi, Pamunkey, Chickahominy, and Appomattox tribes who were able to catch the settlers off guard. Over five hundred settlers were killed in surprise attacks which took place on April 18th. By then, however, the English had grown so numerous in Virginia that, despite the enormous loss of life, the foreigners in Virginia could not be driven out. Elizabeth City County provided men when called upon for attacks made in retaliation. Opechancanough himself was captured and killed. The Algonquian Indians were not a significant threat thereafter.

If the Indian threat receded in the following years, the threat of damage from nature increased. On the 27th day of August, 1667 a hurricane struck the coast of Virginia with a level of force that had not previously been experienced. In Elizabeth City, particularly in the vicinity of the Hampton River, the wind damage was compounded by the storm surge that drove water levels twelve feet above normal. Water levels of that magnitude would have been accompanied by winds in excess of one hundred miles per hour. It is no surprise to read that flimsy buildings of the settlers were destroyed in 1667. Secretary Thomas Ludwell reported:

> "It was the most dreadful hurricane that ever the Colony groaned under."

The rain continued for several days so that the people had to remain in what shelter they could find. They went without food until they were nearly famished. Imagine the scene of devastation when they emerged to find houses destroyed, crops ruined, and drowned people and livestock. Very little escaped the twelve foot floodwaters. The topography of the area was so low and flat that most of the county would have been subject to flooding. Fort Algernon, at Point Comfort, was completely destroyed and had to be abandoned. Thomas Ludwell estimated in a letter that 10,000 houses were blown down.[8] The figure seems excessive but gives an indication of the scope of the calamity. The General Assembly decreed that, because of the loss of crops and livestock, there was a prohibition against the exporting of agricultural products.

The storm was an important consideration in the decision to relocate the church. Less hurricane damage was suffered to the west of the Hampton River, so that construction there was more practical. The center of population at Elizabeth City had been shifting to the west. It was said that in 1667 "there were not fifty able men to bear arms within four miles of the fort at Point Comfort."[9] The General Assembly authorized the residents of Kecoughtan to relocate the church roughly a mile and a half to the west of the second church.[10] In 1667 the new area became the site of the third church.

Eight

The Third Church, 1667

Drawing by Shannon McCall.

The completion of the third church at what was later known as the "Pembroke Plantation" was the culmination of the ministry of the Reverend Justinian Aylmer at Elizabeth City Parish. He must have worked hard to persuade his congregation that the location west of the Hampton River would serve them better. Getting the approval of the General

Assembly to construct a new church no doubt required a proponent like Aylmer who could push the issue until permission was granted to construct a new building and move. Then too, there was the matter of cost to be overcome. The congregation was taxed to pay for the construction of the new building. The church tax, that paid the salary of the minister and the cost of ministering to the poor, was increased by the amount needed to pay for the building.

Having established the new church, Aylmer concluded his twenty-two years of service. There continued to be a shortage of ministers in the colony, however, and he was employed later at the James City Parish. He died there in 1671.

The third church at Elizabeth City, located on the west side of the Hampton River at the "Pembroke Plantation", was built in 1667. It was approximately fifty feet by twenty-seven feet, about the same size as the second church. A factor in its location may have been its proximity to the main roads of Elizabeth City County. It had a brick foundation and was probably similar in appearance to its predecessor. Unlike the second church, it had glass windows. Regrettably, there has not been an archeological exploration at the site of the third church which could provide us more information about this period.

For many years, the second church remained standing. For reasons of convenience or sentiment, it continued to be used, particularly for weddings or funerals. The archeological explorations at the second church resulted in an estimate that at least seventy-five interments were located within the church, some of which occurred after 1667.[1]

Having to make repeated crossings of the Hampton River to reach two church sites may have seemed a burden to the minister who followed Justinian Aylmer. There was a fee of three pence to use the ferry and there were sometimes delays in the ferry service.

The ministry of the next rector, the Reverend Jeremiah Taylor, was not a happy one. Having to occasionally conduct a service at the second church was not the reason. Taylor seems to have been a prime example of the type of man, unfit for ministerial service, who could not find suitable employment in England and made his way to the Virginia Colony. He had a violent temper and was often in trouble with the local authorities. He was brought to court on separate occasions for drunkenness and for slander.

When in the county court, he so upset the justices with his behavior that he was placed in confinement in the county jail.[2] Jeremiah Taylor appeared frequently in court, both civil and criminal, both bringing suit and being sued. Bishop William Meade, writing in 1857, makes the judgment that Taylor was a disgrace to his name and the ministry. Meade was a strong critic of the absence of a bishop in Virginia to watch over the conduct of the clergy, a condition that existed for the entire colonial period.[3]

A few years prior to the construction of the third church, the General Assembly had abrogated the existing laws on the books and had begun afresh with a series of laws intended to replace those that had been enacted as a result of the English Civil War. As in the early days of the colony, precedence was given to the laws related to religion. With the observation "because it is impossible to honor the king as we should unless we serve and fear God," the first twelve acts had to do with religion. The new laws were a reaffirmation of the existing code as it related to building churches, appointing vestries, and conducting services. Included among the acts was a definition of glebes to be established for every parish. The glebe consisted of a house and land for the use of the minister, and was accompanied by a salary of at least eighty pounds per year, or the equivalent in tobacco which amounted to 13,333 pounds weight. It is no surprise that the minister's salary was specified in tobacco because throughout the colonial period England did not provide sufficient currency for the colonists to have any other choice but to resort to barter.

According to the law, ministers had to have been ordained by a bishop in England and subscribed to the laws of the Church of England. Ministers acting in violation of this law were to be silenced by the Governor and sent out of the country.[4]

Government support for religious life was demonstrated not only by legislative action but also by the action of the courts. In providing for the care of orphans, for example, it was common for the court to prescribe religious training. Here in Kecoughtan, Robert Cradocke, at the age of five, was bound as an apprentice to Arnold Jefford and Deborah, his wife, until twenty-one. They were to:

"furnish him meat, drink, washing, and lodging and also to learn him
the Lord's Prayer, the Ten Commandments, and to read a chapter of the

Bible and pay him three barrels of Indian corn and clothing according to custom when free."[5]

The legislature did not show as great an interest in the religious training of Africans as it did of the English. Slave owners were encouraged to have their slaves baptized but they were not penalized if they did not. The religious opportunities a slave might have were up to the owner to decide. The General Assembly decreed that the act of baptism did not provide freedom to the slave.

There were black indentured servants who had served long enough to be free men; and, like other free men had access to the courts. Abraham Saby, a black indentured servant, petitioned the court to be free of the county levy, or tax. He was considered disabled from labor due to his age of one hundred years. Upon consideration of his age, the court granted his request and ordered that in the future Abraham Saby be free from county taxes.[6]

The tranquility of the Virginia Colony was upset by a series of Indian attacks in 1675 along the Potomac. Inaction by Governor Berkeley despite these attacks and others on the western frontier resulted in an uprising in 1676 led by Nathaniel Bacon, Jr. There was little impact on Elizabeth City from Bacon's Rebellion although Elizabeth, the widow of Nathaniel Bacon, later married Thomas Jarvis who operated a trading post in Kecoughtan along the Hampton River.[7]

The precise date of the termination of Jeremiah Taylor's ministry at the third church is unknown. The Reverend William Harris became the next minister in 1675. He served at most for only two years, his successor being appointed in 1677. The Reverend John Page, an Oxford graduate, served until 1687 after which he left the colony.

The Reverend Cope D'Oyley became minister in 1687 but had a short tenure. D'Oyley went on to become minister at Bruton Parish in Williamsburg.

The Reverend James Wallace, a native of Scotland, became minister at Elizabeth City Parish in 1691. Wallace, like Jeremiah Taylor, often appeared in court but he was more likely to be involved in business disputes than the disorderly Taylor. When the number of actions against Wallace became too burdensome, he went to England and returned with

Graves at the third church including those of the Reverend Andrew Thompson and Peter Heyman who was killed by pirates in 1717.

a government order directing that all suits against him should cease. According to court officials in Elizabeth City, obtaining the government order had made Mr. Wallace insulting as well as scoffing and deriding when he appeared before the court. He apparently had the same effect on people he had sued because he was on one occasion violently assaulted on the courthouse steps by a legal opponent and his son. He served at the third church until his death in 1712.[8]

Although the Anglican ministers in Virginia had no bishop resident in the colony, James Blair of Williamsburg, the first president of the College of William and Mary, held the post of Commissary. As Commissary, he supervised the ministers of the colony and reported to the Bishop of London. Through his personality and long tenure he came to exert a powerful influence. Many of the ministers he recruited for the college were from Scotland, including the contentious James Wallace, rector of the church at Pembroke.

Upon the death of Wallace, it was not surprising that the Reverend Andrew Thompson, another Scot, should be appointed as replacement in 1712. Like his predecessor, he was prone to use the courts, but primarily to enforce church attendance from members of his congregation. Some of them may have found diversions such as horse racing or the taverns that were available at the bustling community of Hampton to be more appealing than church attendance.

On May 17, 1715, at a court held in Hampton, Alexander Avery, John Whitfield, Thomas Taylor and ten other men were present on a charge of not coming to church. The usual fine was fifty pounds of tobacco.[9]

The Reverend Thompson died in 1719 at the age of forty-six. He is characterized as "leaving the character of a sober and religious man."[10] His gravesite is one of the eight that have been identified within the foundation of the church at Pembroke.

Nine

Port Hampton

Historians have written about the desire of Virginians to live apart on plantations and how this practice hindered the formation of towns. Nevertheless, the forces of economics and the continual encouraging of the colonial government gradually resulted in the creation of towns.

The formal recognition of Hampton as a town began in 1680 by an act of the General Assembly. In 1691, Hampton was designated as a port for the purpose of encouraging trade. Hampton was to be one of eight ports, there being one in each of the eight counties. The General Assembly condemned fifty acres of the former Jarvis trading plantation because it was well-situated with respect to the Hampton River. Half acre lots were laid out and by 1693 twenty-six of them had been sold. The principal streets, King and Queen, were named for the reigning British sovereigns, King William and Queen Mary. The layout was simple: the two main streets were perpendicular, with King Street leading directly from their intersection to the waterfront. The cross streets of King and Queen became the center of town.

If the Reverend Aylmer had been blessed with foresight thirty years earlier, he and the vestry could have located the third church nearer the Hampton River. Because the Pembroke church was about a mile to the west caused some Hampton residents to complain later that there was no church in the town. Today a brick wall surrounds the site of the Pembroke Church, protecting it from the busy flow of nearby traffic. Within the ancient foundation of the church are eight impressive grave markers. Among those buried there are: Admiral John Neville who died in 1697, Thomas Curle who died in 1700, Peter Heyman who was killed in 1700, the Reverend James Wallace who died in 1712, and the Reverend Andrew Thompson who died in 1719.

Thomas Curle, whose name appears in Elizabeth City Court records, is identified as "gent." on his grave marker. Records show that he purchased a lot in the town of Hampton in 1693 and later became a justice of the Elizabeth City Court.[1]

The circumstances surrounding the death of Peter Heyman are of interest for what they tell about conditions in Hampton in 1700. Shipping at that time was threatened by pirates and privateers who would seize English and colonial vessels that were not protected by an escort. Large shipping convoys would therefore gather in Hampton Roads before sailing to England with British Naval ships as escorts. Armed with thirty guns, the British warship *Shoreham* was stationed at Point Comfort in April, 1700.

Governor Nicholson was in Hampton when it was reported that the French privateer, *La Paix,* was sighted in Lynhaven Bay. Nicholson ordered Captain Passenger of the *Shoreham* to attack the French ship. Aboard as observers were Governor Nicholson and Peter Heyman, the local collector of customs. Thirty-nine of the French were killed in the fighting before the French were forced to strike their colors. One hundred and two French prisoners were taken to Hampton where three were tried and hanged with the remainder sent to England in chains.

Unfortunately, Peter Heyman was killed during the sea battle while standing next to Governor Nicholson. His grave maker, provided by the governor has badly deteriorated. It read, in part:

> "...went voluntarily on Board ye Kings
> shipp Shoreham in Pursuit of a
> Pyrate who greatly infested this
> coast after he had behaved himself
> seven hours with undaunted courage
> was killed with small shot on ye 29th
> Day of April 1700..." [2]

Besides testifying to the devotion of Peter Heyman, this excerpt from the tombstone suggests the magnitude and value of colonial shipping that attracted privateers bold enough to do battle with Royal Navy ships.

The threat of piracy did not end with the defeat of the privateer *La Paix*. In 1718, Edward Teach, better known as Blackbeard the Pirate, was terrorizing the southeast coast of the colonies. Governor Spotswood, in a manner similar to his predecessor Governor Nicholson, dispatched two ships, under the command of Lieutenant Robert Maynard of the Royal Navy, to engage Blackbeard. After a ferocious fight in Pamlico Sound near Ocracoke, North Carolina, Maynard and his crew finally killed Blackbeard after inflicting numerous wounds. He returned to Hampton with the severed head of Blackbeard displayed on the bowsprit of his ship. There was a grand reception for Maynard and his men. Cheering crowds lined the shore and cannons were fired in celebration. As a reminder to would be pirates of the swift system of justice in colonial Virginia, Blackbeard's head was left on public display at the mouth of the Hampton River. Ever since, the land where his head was displayed has been known as Blackbeard's Point.

The large shipping convoys convening in Hampton Roads were not made up of ships from Hampton only. Ships would have come from other ports and trading plantations to Hampton Roads which was the logical place to gather the vessels before beginning their transatlantic crossing. Hampton provided cargos, manpower, and supplies that ships needed for their journey.

Peter Heyman was the designated Naval Officer for the Port of Hampton for the two years preceding his death. The law required each ship entering Hampton harbor to register with the Naval Officer who inspected its cargo. Each ship also paid the port the duties required by the Crown. The successors of Peter Heyman collected these duties until the Revolution.

Hampton was the largest of the designated Virginia ports, each of which had a collector of duties. Its boundaries extended to Archers Creek near Jamestown on the north side of the James and to Hog Island on the south side. Tobacco was the principal export from Hampton. Corn, wheat, hemp, hams and other commodities were also loaded here for destinations at other colonial ports or England. The amount of trade involved made

Hampton Virginia's chief trade center and port of debarkation.[3]

The bustling port required more facilities. A new court house was built in 1716 on land purchased from William Boswell. In 1721, the citizens asked the General Assembly for authority to build a public wharf at the foot of King Street. The wharf was one hundred twenty feet long and eighteen feet wide.[4] These are the approximate dimensions of the wharf in use at that location to this day. Wars and fires have swept away other structures but the King Street wharf remains. There were a number of private wharves as well.

Ordinaries and taverns had proliferated in Hampton from its earliest days. At times the General Assembly saw fit to restrict the number of ordinaries. Some establishments thrived on the trade of thirsty sailors. Others were more respectable and afforded a place for merchants and plantation owners to meet with ship captains for the conduct of business. Prominent among the latter taverns were *The Bunch of Grapes* and *The King's Arms* which were popular gathering places for townspeople and visitors.

Commerce flourished at the port of Hampton.

Ten

The Fourth Church, 1728

Drawing by Shannon McCall.

We gain some knowledge about the conditions in the parish from the report of the Reverend James Falconer who succeeded Andrew Thompson in 1720. In a report to Bishop Gibson in London, Falconer said that he had three hundred fifty families in his charge at the Pembroke church, that service was performed every Sunday, that most of the parishioners attended services, that the Pembroke Church had about one hundred communicants, that the owners of slaves were careful to instruct the young negro children and bring them to baptism, that the minster's salary was about sixty-five pounds, that there were two public schools and one private one in the parish.[1]

Considering the requirement to attend services and the penalties that could be imposed on those who did not attend, it is difficult to understand why services were not attended by all rather than most of the parishioners. Probably relatively long distances and the poor road conditions resulted in some parishioners attending the minimum number of services necessary to avoid being penalized.

There was another reason for non-attendance at Anglican services. In 1699 the Religious Toleration Act was passed by the General Assembly which permitted dissenters to worship in their own way. Even so, the dissenter had to attend the alternative church he had chosen; he could not be a dissenter and opt out of church attendance entirely. Moreover, he was still required to pay the parish levy which supported the Anglican Church and the charitable services it performed such as providing for the poor.

George Walker, a Virginia pilot living in Hampton, was a Quaker whose wife Anne was the daughter of an Anglican minister. She refused to join him at the Quaker services and argued with him over which church their children should attend. The dispute grew to such proportions that she referred the matter to the Council of the Virginia Colony. The council concluded that George Walker should not prohibit his wife from attending Anglican services. With regard to the children the court wisely decided to leave the question unanswered as to which church they should attend.

Margaret Walker, one of the children of George and Anne Walker, later married Thomas Wythe III, a member of the General Assembly. Their son George Wythe was born in 1726 and later became famous as a jurist and signer of the Declaration of Independence.[2]

By the 1720s Hampton was an established town of about one hundred houses. People were complaining, however, about the distance of a mile separating the town from the church at Pembroke Plantation. In addition, people were complaining about the run-down condition of the church. Why not build a church in the town? There were, as usual,

The fourth church was completed in 1728. Its steeple was added in 1762.

people who felt differently and the matter was referred to the Council which concluded that:

> "It is the Opinion of the Board that the New Church should be built in the town of Hampton as the most convenient place in the said Parish and that the Vestry be at liberty to proceed to the building of the same."

Subsequently, the court at Hampton ordered Jacob Walker and John Lowry to lay off an acre and a half of land at the upper end of Queen Street, adjoining the lot of Mr. Boswell, for the building of the new church. The Vestry and Wardens of the Church then entered into an agreement with Henry Cary to furnish him wood to be used in the firing of brick for the church. The wood was cut from the land of the Syms-Eaton School which was administered by the minister, churchwardens and county commissioners.

The bricks for the church were of a style popular in England, giving rise to the rumor that the bricks were imported. Actually, the clay for the bricks was dug at the church lot and the pits were still visible many years later.

As he made brick and erected walls in 1728, Henry Cary could not have known that those same walls would withstand the onslaught of three wars during the next century and a half. None of the earlier churches, made of framed wooden construction, could have survived wars and later been restored. The walls of the fourth church have a thickness of two feet, the length of 2 ½ bricks. It is because of the thickness of these walls and the quality of their construction that the fourth church could be restored. The walls were laid in Flemish bond above the water table with glazed headers. The foundation was laid in English bond. Rubbed brick was used around the curves of windows and at the corners of the church.[3]

The colonial builders laid out a structure in the form of a Latin cross, with the chancel at the east end and an overall length of seventy-five feet, two inches. The transept wings form the arms of the cross which total sixty feet, eight inches. The body of the church and the transept wings are each thirty feet, four inches wide. There were entrances constructed at the west end of the nave and at each end of the transept. The vestibules at each entrance and the tower at the northeast end are later additions. When viewed from either exterior or within, the building overall gives the impression of solidarity. Later changes to the church interior have had little effect on either the materials or the appearance of the exterior.

In 1727 the Reverend Thomas Peador had become rector of the fourth church. As the new building was completed and put into use, he must have shared the enthusiasm and anticipation of his congregation. Upon entering the church for the first time, the worshippers would have noted the plain glass windows that provided most of the illumination of the nave, transepts and chancel. If church members had subscribed to a pew they would have walked over the clay floor tiles in the aisles and opened the door to their box style pew. On the north wall of the nave, just west of the north transept was a small window illuminating the pulpit. Overhead they would have seen three galleries in the north, south and west wings. Above the galleries and the nave was a flat ceiling. There was probably a choir in the north gallery with accompaniment provided by a flutist.[4]

Peter Pelham, a talented organist and composer, came to Hampton in the 1750s and taught music on nearby plantations. Two of his children were born in Hampton so he undoubtedly attended church here; but, the church being without an organ, Pelham went to Williamsburg where he helped install a new organ at Bruton Parish Church. He had a long and distinguished musical career in Williamsburg during the remainder of the eighteenth century.[5]

The fourth church was built in a period of relative stability for the Anglican Church in America. The report submitted by the Reverend James Falconer to Bishop Gibson was also submitted by twenty-eight other Virginia clergy. In their report was information on the length of service of these rectors in their parishes. While the length of service varied from less than three years to over thirty, the average time of clergy in office was twenty-one years at the time the reports were submitted. One cannot help concluding that the rectors were finding contentment in the Virginia ministries.[6]

The Reverend Peador, however, served for only four years in the newly completed church. His successor was William Fyfe who kept "a good private school" in Hampton. His students received instruction in Latin and Greek, in addition to the reading, writing, and arithmetic that formed the entire curriculum of the public schools. James Falconer had described Fyfe as "a man of good life and conversation." It is likely that William Fyfe continued to tutor pupils during his years as minister of the fourth church. His tenure was more similar to the norm among Virginia rectors, extending for twenty-four years until his death in 1755.[7]

William Fyfe's service extended through a busy but peaceful period. Hampton still enjoyed the commerce of a port although depth limitations were causing more and more shipping to use the facilities of Norfolk. Depth limitations, however, were not so shallow that they kept worshippers from coming to church by boat. This practice was continued for generations, and the south door of the church was known as the "water door". The town enjoyed the services of a variety of tradesmen including carpenters, joiners, sawyers, shipwrights, glaziers, shoemakers, and a jeweler. In 1737, in keeping with the status of Hampton as a town, the justices of the court in Hampton ordered that the constable should "kill all the hogs that come within the limits of the town," Nearby plantations provided a foundation for wealth even though tobacco farming had moved further up the rivers of the Tidewater region. Relations with the royal government had not become strained as they were to do in the years preceding the American Revolution.

Jacob Heffelfinger, in his 1910 history of St. John's Church, offers an attractive description of the scene at the church on a Sunday morning. Besides the townsfolk who could now easily walk to the church, there would be an impressive gathering of coaches along Queen Street.

> "Here came the Carys from their "Celey" plantation, the Lowerys and the Mallorys from the Back River, the Barrons from "little England", the Seldens from Buckroe, and others of equal note in the community. Four-in-hand coaches, manned by their liveried black drivers and footmen, and escorted by the country beaux on horseback, rolled up to the church yard gate, there depositing their fair burdens."[8]

Wilson Miles Cary was a wealthy landowner who played a prominent role in public affairs. He was a member of the House of Burgesses and in 1769 became collector of customs at the port.[9] His daughter Sally was one of the belles of Virginia society. Sally Cary and her sisters would have sat with their parents in their pew at the fourth church in Hampton. Sally married William Fairfax, the wealthiest man in Virginia and befriended George Washington who was employed by Fairfax to survey his vast estates.

The church continued to be a gathering place for the community. Announcements were made, news was exchanged, men consulted on the price of crops and dates of ship departures. There was conversation about the relative speed and the quality of horses. All this took place outside the church. Inside were the familiar prayers, psalms set to music, and sermons addressing the morality of the people, past and present.

Eleven

The Approaching Conflict

In 1734 the General Assembly passed a measure requiring that the sheriff pull down all the wooden chimneys in Hampton.[1] This obvious respect for the danger of fires was probably based on the disastrous experience of Jamestown where much damage had been done by fire. The Virginia Colony appreciated the economic value of the town of Hampton, with a probable population of one thousand. Within Elizabeth City County there was an estimated population of four thousand, based on the number of persons on the tax rolls at that time.[2]

In 1749 another hurricane struck that did great damage to Fort George at Point Comfort. The fort, without a foundation on pilings, was practically destroyed.[3] This was the second occurrence of a hurricane sufficiently violent to cause the fort at the entrance to Hampton Roads to be abandoned. Both the tobacco warehouse and the public pier at Hampton sustained great damage and had to be replaced. The vestry had cause to be thankful for the sturdy construction of the fourth church for which no damage was recorded.

In the middle years of the eighteenth century the religious affiliations of the Virginia population began to change. The Scotch-Irish who entered the western part of the commonwealth from Pennsylvania were largely Presbyterian. The religious movement known as the Great Awakening brought more. Baptists began to arrive in the 1740s and their numbers increased greatly in the following decades. The subsequent weakening of support for the established church was felt everywhere in Virginia but less in the Tidewater area.[4]

The earliest vestry records in the possession of the church date from 1751. Examples of entries in the vestry book include:

> On October 17, 1751, it is recorded that five pounds were paid to John Henry Rombough for painting the church.
>
> On the same date, 16,000 pounds of tobacco were levied on the congregation for the annual salary of the Reverend Fyfe.
>
> On November 13, 1751, sixteen shillings and six pence were paid to Captain King "for necessaries for the man with the smallpox."[5]

The major duty that occupied the vestry was caring for the sick and the poor. In Elizabeth City Parish the vestry appointed Dr. Brodie to provide treatment for the poor over a period of many years. When epidemics of smallpox occurred, the vestry provided a pest house, medical supplies, and even coffins when necessary for the deceased. The vestry also would find homes for poor widows and orphans and provide an allowance to the head of the household for their needs.[6]

The first major improvement to the church was made possible by the will of Alexander Kennedy who left forty pounds for the purchase of a church bell, with the provision that the tower had to be completed within one year after his death. At that time the church had no vestibules so the addition of a brick tower eighteen feet square created a vestibule at the west entrance where the tower was built. The tower had walls of the same thickness as the church and a wooden belfry on top. Painted white except for a lead-colored roof, the belfry was originally open but later was enclosed with shutters. In 1765 the church employed Edward Butler to be the "bellman". His salary was one thousand pounds of tobacco per year.

In 1768 the vestry ordered the wardens to "send home for ornaments for the church." The vestry ordered cloth for the pulpit, another cloth for the communion table, and kneeling cushions. All were to be of crimson velvet with a silk fringe. These were the last improvements before the Revolution. Fourteen thousand pounds of tobacco were levied against the congregation to pay for these decorations. Vestryman Wilson Miles Cary agreed to underwrite the shipping costs.[7]

William Selden's application and eventual appointment to be the rector of the church at Hampton portends the eventual breaking away of the colonies from England. Selden was a young lawyer who felt the calling to become an Anglican priest. This was not easy because he had to be ordained by the Bishop of London. Before he could be ordained, he had to have an appointment to a parish.

When the Reverend Fyfe died in 1755, a new rector was needed at Hampton and William Selden sought the appointment. But the Royal Governor, Robert Dinwiddie, chose to exercise his right to nominate the new minister and proposed the name of Thomas Warrington. The vestry then had to choose between the two with the result of a split vestry, half preferred Warrington and half Selden. The issue was eventually resolved in the favor of the Reverend Thomas Warrington.

Selden had to wait if he wished to become the minister at Hampton. Thomas Warrington, however, served as rector until his death in 1770. It was not until then that the position was vacant and William Selden could make the trip to London. He returned from London with the proper credentials and became rector in 1771. The certificate attesting to his ordination on March 10th of that year is preserved in the museum of St. John's Church.[8]

During the twelve years of William Selden's appointment there were incendiary events in the American colonies, events that led to the war with England. One was at Concord, in Massachusetts. Another which involved an aroused population, was at Hampton. The Reverend Selden was a strong supporter of the Revolution and probably did much to stimulate the people in their break with England. His dislike of British rule had begun in the opposition of the royal governor to Selden's appointment to the church in Hampton.

George Wythe was another native of Hampton who raised his voice in opposition to British rule. In 1726 he was born at "Chesterville", the plantation of his father Thomas Wythe III. His father was a vestryman of the church in Hampton.[9] After the death of Thomas Wythe, George was educated by his mother. He received his law training from his uncle. At the age of twenty he began practice of the law in Hampton where he later became one of the justices. While living in Williamsburg he taught law to Thomas Jefferson and John Marshall and became a vestryman at

*George Wythe began his
practice of law in Hampton.*

Bruton Parish Church. In 1765 he won election over Captain James Wallace and Wilson Miles Cary to be a member of the House of Burgesses for Elizabeth City County.[10] He later was a signer of the Declaration of Independence.

Virginia felt the burden of English misrule as did the other colonies. The Stamp Act was an example of taxation without representation whereby colonists were expected to pay a tax on practically every written document. This tax would have been especially odious in a town like Hampton with its many port transactions. Hampton also had a court with its multitude of wills, deeds, and contracts. Elizabeth City County joined in the general boycott of the Stamp Act which then became ineffective. When the act was repealed it was recorded in the *Virginia Gazette* that there was revelry on the night of June 4, 1767, at *The Bunch of Grapes* tavern on King Street. The celebration continued with a dinner and ball at *The King's Arms* tavern across the street.[11]

By 1775, sentiment about British rule had deteriorated considerably. Lord Dunmore, the royal governor, allowed his naval vessels to commandeer poultry and livestock from farms on the north side of Hampton Roads where the population was less likely to be loyalist. These acts naturally added to the resentment felt against the Crown. Some depredations against the people took place near Hampton. The aggressive reactions of the Virginians infuriated Captain Squiers of the Royal Navy. Anticipating a British attack, the men of Hampton sank five vessels in the channel to hinder the approach by water.

With his ship unable to get past the vessels sunk in the channel on October 24, 1775, Captain Squiers sent men in small boats to attack the town. Meanwhile his ship fired cannon in their support. Sharpshooters along the shore were able to drive off the small boats but the cannon fire did some damage to buildings of Hampton. Fortunately, the damage to the church was not severe.

News of the attack reached Williamsburg the same day and one hundred mounted riflemen of the Culpeper militia set out for Hampton. Under the command of Colonel William Woodford, the troops arrived in time to take up positions along the waterfront. On October 25, Captain Squiers cleared the approach channel and sent a schooner, two sloops, and two tenders into the Hampton River from which they fired on the streets of the town. The British would have destroyed the town had it not been for the resistance from the men along the shore. The fire of the Virginia riflemen made it impossible for the gunners on the vessels to keep up their fire. They were forced to withdraw with two men dead, two wounded, seven taken prisoner, and one tender captured by the Americans.[12]

The Battle of Hampton was of little significance militarily. It did, however, show that the colonists were capable of effective military opposition to British rule. Thomas Jefferson said:

"The Battle of Hampton had all Virginia in a frenzy."

Later, after the signing of the Declaration of Independence, lightning struck the tower of the church, knocking down the insignia of English royalty that had adorned it.[13] To many, this "act of God" must have seemed a prophetic omen.

The people of Hampton had little inkling of what lay ahead for them and their neighbors because of the difficulties that had arisen in their relations with England. Nor did they foresee the impact that revolution would have upon their church.

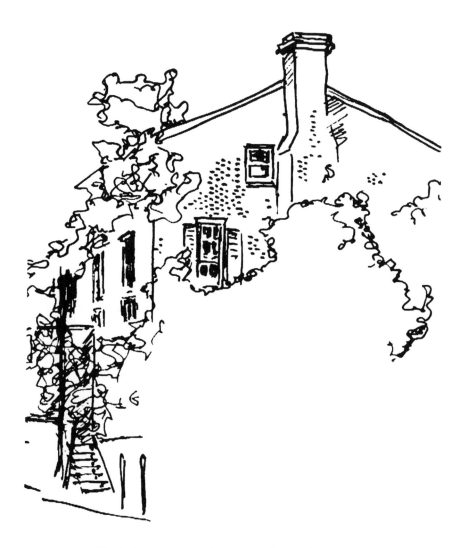

*King's Arms tavern on lower King Street where patriots
met to celebrate the repeal of the Stamp Act in 1767.*

Twelve

The Revolution

In the debates of the Continental Congress leading up to the signing of the Declaration of Independence, the voice and reason of George Wythe had been compelling. He had said it was a "certain position in law that allegiance and protection are reciprocal, the one ceasing when the other is withdrawn."[1] This description of the broken relationship between England and the colonies won the admiration of John Adams. The delegation from Virginias felt such respect for Wythe that they insisted he be the first Virginian to sign the Declaration of Independence.

At the beginning of the Revolution, there were both patriots and Tories in Hampton as there were in most communities. Members of local families had provided leadership for Hampton and its church before the war. They provided leadership again during the war. Besides men who served in the army, a large number of men from Hampton served in the Virginia Navy. Hampton became the headquarters of that Navy which was controlled by a board of commissioners under Colonel Thomas Whiting.

The shipbuilding skills available at Hampton were put to use. At the shipyard near the King Street wharf, a variety of vessels were built for the Virginia Navy. These ranged from armed pilot boats to the *Gloucester* that carried thirty-two guns. Virginia ships were sent out to capture British merchant ships as well as to protect the Virginia coast from marauding British or Tory ships. Ships of the Virginia Navy also carried tobacco to the West Indies to exchange for military supplies.[2]

Salt was a basic commodity not easy to come by in the colonies. For years it was produced from the distillation of seawater by John Cary at his salt works near Buckroe. During the Revolution its production was important enough to warrant a militia guard at the area that is still known as the Salt Ponds.[3]

It must have been an exciting time to live in Hampton. Besides the constant coming and going of ships in the navy that numbered seventy before the end of the war, there was the constant manning of lookouts at Point Comfort to warn of enemy activity.[4] Young boys could linger at the waterfront in hopes of hearing of an encounter returning seamen might have had with an English ship. From the pulpit of the church, the Reverend Selden preached strongly in support of the patriot cause.

To some, the burden of the annual church levy must have been onerous. Besides taxing citizens for assistance to the poor, the levy taxed to pay the minister's salary and raised money to maintain the church buildings. This situation seemed intolerable to the growing number of Virginians who did not support the established church. By the beginning of the Revolution they possessed the political power to do something about it. The Exemption Act of the General Assembly in October, 1776, clearly removed any support for the Virginia church by dissenters:

> "That all dissenters of whatever denomination, from the said church shall be free from and after the passing of the act, be totally free and exempt from all levies, taxes, and impositions whatever, towards supporting and maintaining said church, as it is now or hereafter may be established, and its ministers."

After 1776, care for the poor was continued, but the support of ministers and facilities did not. The act, however, did not require the church to give up any of its property. Although the Reverend Selden continued to serve, he received no pay. He was able to earn income from individual services and from the instruction of private pupils at his home.[5]

Hampton contributed not only ships and sailors to the war; there were many capable naval commanders. Two of these were the brothers Richard and James Barron, members of the church at Hampton.[6] At different times during the war the brothers each commanded the ships *Liberty* and

Patriot which participated in numerous engagements. In the course of the war the *Liberty* survived twenty engagements. Captain James Barron distinguished himself by the capture, in 1776, of a boat Lord Dunmore had sent to Maryland. On board was a copy of the orders for the British to attack Charleston, South Carolina. With this information the colonists were able to prepare for the anticipated attack and defeat it.[7]

Other than the naval attack against Hampton in 1775 and a brief occupation in October of 1780, no action was directed at the town. But late in the war there was a fight near Big Bethel. A force of two hundred British was marching from Newport News to Yorktown when they encountered the Elizabeth City militia. Colonel Francis Mallory, leader of the outnumbered forty Americans, charged boldly into the British. He lost his life after suffering numerous wounds.[8] Colonel Mallory was a vestryman of the church at Hampton.

In December 1780, Benedict Arnold sailed into Chesapeake Bay in command of a force of British troops. Hampton was fortunate not to be the target of raids that were intended to remove the South from the war. The British commanders Arnold and Cornwallis were unsuccessful in destroying American resistance. While no decisive battles were fought here, Cornwallis eventually maneuvered himself into a corner at Yorktown from which he was not able to escape. Men from the Hampton militia were at Yorktown to participate in the final victory of the Americans and French.

After the surrender of Lord Cornwallis at Yorktown, a French officer, Captain Dee Blondeau, the commander of the "Lauzan Legion", gave a large prayer book to the Reverend William Selden. With the inscription "Dee Blondeau of Duke Lauzan Legion to the Rev. William Selden", the prayer book was handed down through the family to Selden's great-great-granddaughter, Mary Selden. In 1950, she presented the book to St. John's Church where it is displayed in the church museum.[9]

After Yorktown, French soldiers of the Lauzan Legion were billeted in Hampton. These soldiers used the courthouse as a hospital. In order to plan the disposition of three hundred troops billeted here, French cartographers produced the 1781 map of Hampton that has been preserved. A prominent feature on the map is a cross which locates the church.

The Revolution marked changes for the people of Hampton. The shallow draft of the Hampton River, compared with deeper water available at Norfolk, was bringing about a decline in Hampton as a port. The Revolution, which was marked by a loss in trade with the West Indies, greatly reduced what little trade remained. Gone were the days when Hampton was the principal port of Virginia.[10]

Another change in Hampton was shared by all the other communities in Virginia where the Anglican Church had played an important role. The established church, already making way for other denominations, now no longer enjoyed its privileged position. In the new country that had struggled long and hard for freedom, many citizens had little use for what they felt was a religion imposed by the government.

The location of the church in the 1781 French military map
is at the cross just below the south arrow.

View of the north side of the church as it appeared at the time of the Revolution.

Part II
Independence and Wars
1783 - 1865

Thirteen

The Church in Transition

Compared with the damage inflicted on St. John' Church later during the War of 1812 and the Civil War, the harm suffered during the Revolution was minimal. Through political action, however, great loss was imposed upon the established church in Virginia. The church in Hampton had enjoyed the benefits of being a part of the establishment. At the start of the Revolution, the General Assembly, denied churches the right to support the minister and maintain the church building through the use of a church tax on the people. This required the vestry to find an entirely different way to raise the funds necessary for the church. Whereas previously a tax levy was made based on the number of persons eligible to be taxed, a much smaller number of people now contributed voluntarily to the church. In 1783, the vestry asked that each titheable person pay six shillings for the past services of the Reverend Selden who retired at that time. He was the last of the colonial ministers.[1]

The use of the glebe land was still available to the church at Hampton, and the vestry took advantage of this right to contract for the services of the Reverend William Nixon to serve as minister. He was allowed the use of the land and the accompanying slaves for his compensation. He served for one year, after which he departed in 1784 for Baltimore where he opened a classical school.[2]

Examination of the surviving vestry book of the period reveals that a major portion of the vestry activity was taken up with providing for the poor of the parish. In the book are recorded the expenses actually incurred in the support of widows and orphans who had no other means of support. This duty was assumed by a group of Elizabeth City officials designated as the Overseers of the Poor. Since they were probably the same men who were on the vestry, the vestry book was turned over to them. Another book, not available to us, was used for whatever meetings the vestry may have held. In 1806, the Overseers of the Poor sold the glebe lands previously belonging to the church. Required by an act of the General Assembly, sale of glebes further diminished the financial health of what was formerly the established church.[3]

Because of its ties to England, resentment toward the church following the Revolution was understandable. Considered along with the actions of the General Assembly to confiscate the glebes, this attitude appeared harsh and even spiteful. It is a wonder that the church survived. The seizure of the glebes had a disastrous effect on the Episcopal churches in Virginia because the glebes had been the primary means of support for the minister. Many churches were no longer able to continue. In those cases, the church buildings themselves were also seized and used by other denominations or for secular purposes. By 1811, only forty of the 107 Anglican parishes existing in 1784 were still able to support ministers. The remainder ceased to exist.[4]

In 1788, the justices of Elizabeth City County rebuked the board of trustees of the church for letting "the horses and cattle run in the church yard."[5] Sometime after 1806, the church bell had to be removed from its tower because the wood of the tower had rotted and there was not enough money for repairs. The bell was placed at ground level in the angle made by the church and the tower.[6] How this state of affairs must have appalled parishioners who remembered prosperity of the church!

Another difficulty that followed the Revolution was the inability of the church in America to look any longer to England for bishops who could ordain ministers. Fortunately, there were able men in America who took action in securing bishops. The first General Convention of the Episcopal Church in the United States of America met in Philadelphia on September 27, 1785. The convention began work on a constitution for the newly named Episcopal Church. Work also began on revision of the *Book of Common Prayer* and a plan for the consecration of bishops. The

Archbishops of Canterbury and York were willing to consecrate American bishops. Among the first three ministers who were elected by their states to go to England for consecration was James Madison of Virginia. He was consecrated as Bishop of Virginia in 1790.[7]

Bishop James Madison, whose second cousin by the same name became fourth president of the United States, was clearly qualified to lead the diocese that chose him to be its leader. At the age of forty-one, he possessed the zeal needed to undertake the momentous challenge of the revival of a moribund church. He made visitations to numerous parishes, confirmed hundreds, and recruited more new ministers than any of the seven other American bishops.

Despite the fact that he was the Rector of James City Parish as well as the President of the College of William and Mary, Bishop Madison did not have the aid of an assistant bishop. Needless to say, he was overloaded. In 1805, he was ill with dropsy and went into virtual retirement as Bishop of Virginia.[8] At his death in March 1812, the church in Virginia was described as being in "freefall".

During some of this difficult period for the church, the Episcopal church at Hampton managed to fill its pulpit. The Reverend William Bland came after the Reverend Nixon and, in 1786, served as a delegate to the convention of the diocese. He was succeeded by the Reverend Henry Skyren, a minister who was of English birth. After serving other churches in King William and in King and Queen Counties, Mr. Skyren was called to Hampton. The people of Hampton were fortunate to have him because he was noted for his eloquence as well as his piety. He drew large congregations to hear him preach. After his death in 1795 he was followed by the Reverend John Jones Spooner. A Harvard graduate, Mr. Spooner had served with distinction in the militia of the state of Massachusetts after the Revolution. Following his death in 1799, the position of minister was filled by the Reverend Benjamin Brown.

The Reverend Brown, who had previously been minister at St. Peter's church in New Kent County, served at Hampton until his death in 1806.[9] There is a legend that his wife, Rachel C. Garrett of Hampton, had married Count Rochambeau when the French Army was garrisoned in the town. When she returned to France with him, she was disillusioned to learn that he was already married and consequently returned to Hampton.[10]

The graves of the Reverends Skyren, Spooner, and Brown are in the cemetery of St. John's Church.

In the years preceding the War of 1812, the church at Hampton, like so many Episcopal churches was unable to employ a minister. The Reverend Seymour Symms was elected rector in 1806 but did not serve because there was no provision for his pay. Likewise, the Reverend George Holson was elected in 1810 but did not serve.[11] The church at Hampton suffered from the same malaise that oppressed her sister churches throughout the state of Virginia.

Fourteen

The War of 1812

It was often necessary in the early 1800s for lay persons to conduct services because the church was unable to support a regular minister. Ministers could have been employed for single services such as marriages. Indeed, the Reverend George Holson, for whom the church was unable to provide a salary, was employed nearby in a school at Hampton. Although only a clergyman could administer Holy Communion, lay persons could lead Morning and Evening Prayer which were available in the *Book of Common Prayer* for use in either the church or the home.

In the meantime, the church building continued to deteriorate. The memory of better days and hope for a restoration must have sustained those who eventually would respond to the call to restore the old church in the faith community.

There was to be a change in the system of free schools that had been established by the wills of Benjamin Syms and Thomas Eaton. In 1805 there were no churchwardens who had shared in the administration of the schools. The schools had fallen into disrepair and the Eaton school was not operating. The General Assembly authorized the sale of the Syms and Eaton properties in order to create a fund that would establish a secondary school in Hampton. By 1810, the Hampton Academy was in operation on Cary Street. To the people of the community, the Hampton Academy offered a educational opportunity for their children that was superior to the hiring of private tutors and poor children could attend without charge. There was a faculty that could prepare students for attendance at the College of William and Mary. [1]

One of the events leading to the War of 1812 was the firing of the British ship *Leopard* on the American ship *Chesapeake* on June 22, 1807. James Barron, a member of the Barron family of Hampton, was Commodore in command of the *Chesapeake*. Barron was tried by court martial and convicted of not preparing his ship for combat. He was suspended from the service for five years but later he was restored to active duty.

During the War of 1812, Commodore Lewis Warrington, grandson of Thomas Warrington, a past rector of the church at Hampton, distinguished himself in naval operations. His ship, the *Peacock*, engaged the British sloop, *Epervier*, which was convoying a group of merchantmen. When the British ship surrendered, she was found carrying 118,000 pounds in coined money. On the same cruise Warrington's ship captured a total of fourteen British merchantmen. [2]

Hampton, where damage had been slight during the Revolution, did not fare as well during the War of 1812. Rear Admiral Sir George Cockburn of the Royal Navy was the commander of the British forces. He planned to attack Norfolk. But first he had to take the American fort at Craney Island which protected the entrance to the Elizabeth River. The defenders at Craney Island drove off the attackers with direct artillery fire that inflicted heavy losses. The British withdrew and decided not to attempt another attack up the Elizabeth River. [3] Looking about for an objective where he might be more successful, Admiral Cockburn chose the small town of Hampton. He could either attack up the Hampton River or land forces on the northern shores of Hampton Roads and advance on the town. The American militia of 436 men was encamped at "Little England" near the mouth of the Hampton River on the west bank. On the morning of June 25, Cockburn approached the mouth of the Hampton River and fired on the American encampment. Simultaneously, the main British force, in excess of 2,000 men, landed near the Cary plantation at "Celey", about two miles to the west. The Americans moved to meet the British force.

With no chance of success, the initial American fusillade was met with a seemingly unending musket fire. In the words of American Captain Cooper who witnessed the action. The pounding of English muskets was "like the roll of twenty drums." Soon in retreat, the Americans managed to evade attempts to encircle them. They withdrew toward Yorktown, leaving open the road to Hampton.

The Battle of Hampton in the War of 1812 was memorable for the deplorable lack of control exercised by the British commander over his men when they occupied the town. The helpless citizens were subjected to robbery, rape, and murder. British Lieutenant Colonel Charles Napier wrote of his commander, "Colonel Beckwith ought to have hanged several villains, every horror was committed...and not a man was punished."[4]

The Episcopal Church was used as barracks for soldiers and the churchyard for the slaughtering of animals. Fortunately, the British remained in Hampton for only a few days because they heard rumors of an approaching American army. They returned to their ships by July 1, 1813. The town was not burned, probably because of the precipitous departure. But much damage was done to objects which could not be taken. The old church, which previously had been neglected, was now a ruin. It had even lost its bell which had been removed to the American campground at "Little England". Before the battle the church bell had been used as a dinner bell. The bell was useless, having cracked when struck with a hammer.[5]

Although the British remained at Hampton only a few days, they proved to be efficient looters. There was said to be scarcely a silver knife, fork or piece of plate left in Hampton.[6] Whoever concealed the church's communion silver to prevent it from being stolen was never revealed..

After the war, the Federal Government compensated the citizens for losses they suffered. The claims of persons who had lost possessions, including personal property, ships or slaves were paid. Compensation was even received for the cracked church bell.[7]

Nothing was done, however, to restore the church in the period of religious apathy that followed the War of 1812. George Mason writes that, "A dozen years of such neglect reduced the structure to four walls and a leaky roof, without doors, windows, floors, or other interior woodwork, while the decayed timbers of the belfry on the steeple fell down and were carried off with the rest."[8]

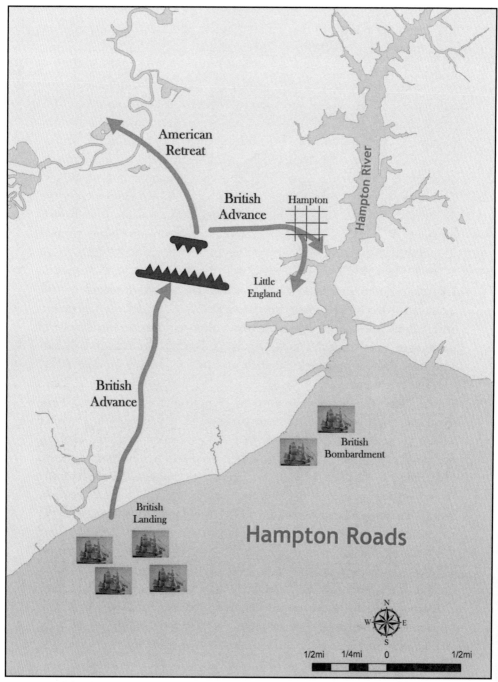

British landing and battle at Hampton on June 25, 1813 followed by sack of the town.

Fifteen

The Restoration

The support and prayers of many people were involved in the restoration of the church which had been so abused in the War of 1812 and neglected in the years that followed. Two persons played prominent roles of encouragement distinguishing them from the many who provided support.

The first was Mrs. Jane Barron Hope, daughter of Commodore James Barron. She spoke words that were long remembered and preserved from a letter written later by Mr. Richard B. Servant, a young man living in Hampton,

"In the year 1822 or 1823, just as I was arriving to manhood, an incident occurred that I shall never forget. Mrs. Jane Hope, eldest daughter of the late Commodore James Barron, was spending the evening with my mother, (who resided on the lot adjoining, west of the church,) and she proposed a visit to the graves of our ancestors; and, while standing at

Mrs. Jane Barron Hope whose words inspired the restoration of the church.

the front door of the church, within a foot of the graves of my ancestors, she remarked to me, '**Cousin, if I were a man I would have these walls built up.**' Her words were like electricity, and from that moment my determination was fixed."

The following day, Richard Servant went to call upon community leaders who decided to undertake the repair of the walls of the churchyard. After soliciting the commitments of persons in Hampton, Servant went to Norfolk where he found others sympathetic to the cause. Enough money was raised to repair the walls and erect a substantial wrought iron gate at the entrance.[1]

With the walls restored, there was a growing desire to rehabilitate the church building that had been in a dilapidated condition for so long. In August of 1826, a group of citizens "friendly to the Episcopal Church" met at the Hampton court house and elected a vestry. At subsequent meetings, committees were formed to raise funds and to call on Bishop Moore.

Bishop Richard Channing Moore was the second person who gave special encouragement to the restoration. Consecrated Bishop of Virginia in 1814, Moore had done much to resuscitate the ailing Episcopal Church in Virginia which had been virtually leaderless due to the long illness of Bishop Madison. By 1814, there were only nineteen Episcopal churches in Virginia that had settled ministers. Bishop Moore had the experience and the ability to respond to the challenge to restore decaying churches. He traveled throughout Virginia to consecrate churches, confirm new members, and ordain ministers. He encouraged the growth of Sunday schools which were largely taught by women.[2] The church at Hampton was destined to be the object of his attention.

Bishop Moore promised to visit Hampton and provide counsel. In his letter to the vestry he said,

"To see the temple repaired in which the former inhabitants of Hampton worshipped God, and to see you placed under the care of a faithful and judicious clergyman, will fill my mind with greatest delight. May God Almighty smile on the proposed design, and carry it into full and complete effect."[3]

The campaign to raise funds "for the repair of the Protestant Episcopal Church in Hampton" resulted in a subscription signed by ninety persons. The contributions ranged from one hundred dollars to forty-seven cents. The largest contribution was received from Commodore James Barron, whose daughter, Mrs. Jane Hope, had made the stirring declaration, "Cousin, if I were a man I would have these walls built up."[4]

The repairs included renewal of the roof and rafters and the installation of new doors, windows, floors, and plastered ceiling. New furniture and pews were installed.

Portrait of Bishop Richard Channing Moore.

The total cost for the repairs was about $1,200. In accordance with the custom of the time, the pews were sold to the highest bidder to help meet expenses. Two pews were left unsold for the use of visitors. A visitor to the church would have seen little difference in the box pews from those which had existed in colonial days. Likewise, red tiles, one and one-half inches thick, were placed directly on the ground to pave the aisles. The pulpit was located differently, however, in the center of the chancel rather than next to the north wall. Fifteen more years were to pass before the wooden belfry was replaced on the church tower.[5]

In June, 1827, Bishop Moore visited Hampton at which time he confirmed twenty-two persons and preached to a large congregation. He later reported,

> "The Church in Hampton had been in a state of ruin for many years, but the inhabitants have now rendered it fit for service, and when the repairs are completed it will form a place of worship inferior to very few in the diocese."

*Portrait of the Reverend Mark
Chevers, about 1830.*

In April, 1827, the Reverend Mark L. Chevers was elected rector by the vestry for the period of one year. Born in 1795, Chevers had served as a sergeant in the War of 1812 and was ordained as priest in 1826. He was reelected Rector of Hampton's Episcopal Church each year until 1843. He had long been known to Bishop Moore who must have been pleased that Chevers was providing the "care of a faithful and judicious clergyman". On March 6,1830, Bishop Moore consecrated the restored church in Hampton under its new name: St. John's.

The Reverend Chevers was a man of remarkable energy and enthusiasm. In 1838 he was appointed as chaplain at Fort Monroe, a position he held concurrently with his ministry at St. John's. He conducted services on Sunday morning at Fort Monroe and at St. John's in the afternoon. Chevers often walked from the fort to the town. Thinking nothing of walking from Hampton to Yorktown, he was preaching on Saturday from house to house at other locations on the Virginia Peninsula, . When his schedule permitted he would walk even to Richmond. Not handicapped by being born before the age of microphones and amplifiers, Chevers had a booming voice. He could preach outdoors as well as indoors. St. John's did not have a proper vesting room for the priests in his day. Not a hardship for a man accustomed to the outdoors, he would put on his robes outdoors in the northeast angle of the church. The Reverend Chevers was present for duty as chaplain at Fort Monroe until his death in 1875. During his ministry the Chapel of the Centurion was built in 1858. For a brief period during the imprisonment of Jefferson Davis at Fort Monroe, Chaplain Chevers ministered to the former president of the Confederacy. He was also active in ministering to the large body of soldiers that flowed through Fort Monroe and the nearby hospitals during the Civil War.

The funeral service for the Reverend Mark Chevers was held at the Chapel of the Centurion on Fort Monroe. After the service the funeral procession proceeded to St. John's cemetery where he was buried with military honors.[6]

The Government of the United States had learned a bitter lesson during the Revolution and The War of 1812: undefended coastlines were vulnerable to attack by maritime powers such as Great Britain. In response to a need to defend our coast, a huge construction program consisting of forty-two forts was authorized. Work began in 1819 at Fort Monroe and in 1830 at Castle Calhoun (later renamed Fort Wool).

By the 1830s a military community was in place. The interaction with Hampton was begun that continues to the present day. The experience of Chaplain Chevers is but one example of the ties between the two communities. The decision to build Fort Monroe at Old Point Comfort would have significant impacts in the coming decades on Hampton and St. John's Church.

*The Chapel of the Centurion was built
at Fort Monroe during the ministry of the Rev. Chevers.*

Sixteen

A Pretty Little Town

The period between the War of 1812 and the Civil War was a time of growth for both St. John's Church and the Diocese of Virginia. Under the able leadership of Bishop Moore the Diocese had instituted a number of supports for the member churches. These supports included the development of Sunday Schools, voluntary societies to organize parish and mission work, the Virginia Theological Seminary to provide a stream of clergymen, and a religious journal.[1]

In 1841 Bishop Moore died after serving the diocese for more than a quarter of a century. He was succeeded by his long-time assistant bishop, William Meade, a man who shared Moore's energy and commitment to the church. Continuing the tradition of having an assistant bishop, the Virginia convention elected Bishop John Johns to the position.

Bishop Meade had a decided view in the contest between high and low church within the Episcopal denomination. He was on the side of low church and the Diocese of Virginia remained an overwhelmingly low church diocese. In Tidewater Virginia this followed a long tradition of Calvinist leanings. On the issue of slavery, he advocated spreading the Gospel to slaves in Virginia but gave no support to the abolition of slavery as an institution. Individual parishes in the Diocese varied in the attention they paid to black parishioners.[2]

Bishop Johns, the assistant bishop, made his first visit to St. John's on April 12, 1843, at which time he confirmed seven. It was the last year of the Reverend Mark Chevers' service at St. John's. A total of thirty communicants were on the rolls. Chevers was followed by John P. Bausman as Rector of St. John's Church.[3] The Reverend Bausman credited the women volunteers of St. John's Church for the effectiveness of their support. The women provided a lecture room in the east or chancel end of the church. They followed this with a fair that netted three hundred fifty dollars to be used for church repairs. At that time the Sunday school was reported to be flourishing.

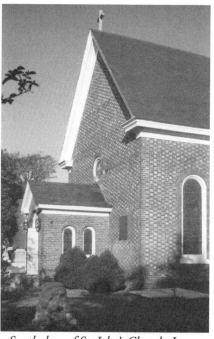

The Reverend William Goode followed John Bausman as rector of St. John's Church in 1845 and served for three years. His last report showed the number of

South door of St. John's Church. It was known as the "water door" in the days when people came to church by boat.

communicants had risen to forty-two.[4] Many of the congregation came to church by means of boats. They could row on the Hampton River to the inlet closest to the south door. In those days much of what has now become landfill was still water so that boats could navigate almost to Queen Street. The intersection of Queen Street and Armistead Avenue was known as Marsh Market Corner where farmers brought their produce for sale. The south door of the church was for many years known as "the water door".

In 1850, the vestry chose as minister the Reverend John C. McCabe, a man of wide ranging interests. He is credited as being an outstanding speaker. He was a writer who had published several books of poetry. McCabe had submitted poetry to Edgar Allan Poe for publication when Poe was editor of *The Messenger.*[5] John McCabe wrote numerous articles about the old churches of tidewater Virginia. St. John's was one of these churches. St. John's Church, at the time of McCabe's ministry, already had a history of almost two hundred fifty years. Well over one hundred years had elapsed since the fourth church had been built in 1728. People unfortunately had forgotten the locations of the previous three churches. McCabe set out to find the third site.

We can sense McCabe's enthusiasm when he writes about discovering the third site,

> "We have only to turn our footsteps to the 'Pembroke Farm' (the property of John Jones, Esq.) about one mile from the town of Hampton, and as we there take our stand among the few remaining tombs, shout "Eureka, Eureka!"

In his article in *International Magazine*, McCabe described the tombstones in detail and show how they are evidence of the third site of the church in Hampton.[6] Today the third site is protected by a wall provided by the Hampton Roads Garden Club in 1950.

Although Hampton had long been eclipsed as a port by nearby Norfolk, maritime activities still were prominent in the community. Shipbuilding continued along the banks of the Hampton River. Many of the maritime pilots were residents of Hampton. These pilots brought ships into Hampton Roads and the rivers of Tidewater Virginia. Many citizens made a living in the harvesting of seafood and the building and repair of boats.

The Army built Castle Calhoun, later renamed Fort Wool, on an artificial island near Fort Monroe. Lt. Robert E. Lee, of the U.S. Army Corps of Engineers, was in charge of the work. The island became a vacation retreat for President Andrew Jackson. The appeal of salt water and a mild climate drew people to the Virginia Peninsula. In 1820, the Hygeia Hotel was built beside Fort Monroe. It became a popular health resort and upscale destination for tourists. Former President John Tyler and his wife Julia enjoyed the society at the Hygeia Hotel and Fort Monroe. The Tylers built a summer home near the Hampton River which they named Villa Margaret. Their youngest child, Pearl, was born there in 1860. The Tylers attended St. John's Church when they were in residence in Hampton but the pew where they sat was not recorded.

There were also educational opportunities available to the families of residents of Hampton. John B. Cary founded the Hampton Military

Academy which drew young men and women from other states as well as Virginia. The Chesapeake Female College was established in an imposing building overlooking Hampton Roads on the site where the first English settlers had landed in 1607.[7]

A glimpse of what was directed toward the minds of students and parents was recorded in an address delivered by the Reverend McCabe to pupils at Hampton Academy on July 30, 1853,

> "If the teaching of the fireside, if the morality of homes is not wrought to bear, the chances are that the seeds sown in the school room will be scorched and withered at the hearth stone. Intellectual education is a gift of great price, but moral is of greater."[8]

During the period of John McCabe's ministry, an organ was purchased for St. John's Church at a cost of $263. The Reverend McCabe was succeeded at St. John's Church in 1856 by the Reverend Edward Harlow. By 1860, the number of communicants was sixty-two. Other churches were flourishing in Hampton. The First Baptist Church was founded in 1791, and the First Methodist Church was founded in 1811.[9]

With a population of about 2,500, the town probably resembled Fredericksburg or Alexandria in the days immediately preceding the Civil War. Beautiful homes with spacious gardens extended along the Hampton River and white-sailed fishing boats plied the waterways. Farm fields planted with golden wheat extended along the roads leading out of town. Travelers along the roads and citizens in town could hear the bell of St. John's Church tolling for weddings, funerals, and calling the faithful to worship.[10]

It was a scene soon to disappear.

Seventeen

The Burning of Hampton

In 1861, Hampton was once again visited by war. Less than half a century had elapsed since the War of 1812 when the church was ruined. In the Civil War the damage to the town was so complete that it had to be entirely rebuilt. In order to convey the magnitude of the forces that were brought to bear on the town and its people, the conditions that existed and events that occurred must be described.

One of the most significant factors affecting Hampton was the proximity of Fort Monroe. After the firing on Fort Sumter in 1861, the Federal Government increased its efforts to protect Fort Monroe. Because they provided a foothold on the Virginia Peninsula, the Federal forces here had enormous strategic significance. Troop reinforcements as well as additional armaments were sent to the fort. By mid-May, over 2,000 troops were on duty under the command of Colonel Justin Dimick.[1] It was only the beginning of the flood of manpower and materiel that would pass through the Fort Monroe.

At the same time when troop strength at Fort Monroe was building up, many of the men of the town of Hampton were being mobilized into local militia units. These units included the Wythe Rifles, the Hampton Grays, and the Old Dominion Dragoons. The military effectiveness of these units varied from company to company. Most of them required a great deal of training before they would become effective. About fifty students from the Hampton Military Academy, as well as several faculty members, eventually enlisted. Their schoolmaster, Major Cary, commanded the local units.

Events were moving rapidly; too rapidly for some. Miss Fanny Worsham of Hampton later recalled,

> "The war came just as suddenly as a flash of lightning. Nobody a month before it started believed for a minute that there'd actually be a war."[2]

The Confederate plan to defend against the Union forces made no attempt to hold the tip of the Peninsula. Fort Monroe was considered to be impregnable. The first Confederate line of defense was about ten miles northwest of Hampton.

Tension increased in May when Federal troops from Fort Monroe seized a well across Mill Creek and the bridge. The troop population at the fort could not be supported by the cisterns they used for water supply. To the local populace the move across Mill Creek seemed like an invasion.

It was followed on May 23rd by an incursion into Hampton by eight hundred troops of the 1st Vermont Infantry. General Benjamin Butler, the new commander at Fort Monroe had sent them to disrupt the vote on secession that was underway in Hampton. Major Cary, in command of a small Confederate force, did not attempt to oppose the Federal troops. The polls were closed, the troops returned to Fort Monroe, and the voting was resumed. The result was overwhelmingly in favor of succession.[3] This event was a demonstration of how vulnerable Hampton was to the troops at Fort Monroe.

With the Union strength at Fort Monroe so apparent and the men of Hampton leaving for military service, many families decided to leave Hampton. They went to Williamsburg, Gloucester, or Richmond, anywhere their resources and family relations permitted. The Reverend William F. Jacobs, minister of St. John's Church in May 1861 reported,

> "Congregation broken up, and some families have gone, we fear, to return no more."[4]

A soldier from Hampton said later,

"...old Hampton, which had for years afforded such pleasant homes for many of us now assumed a sad and lonely appearance..."⁵

James Barron Hope's daughter said,

"My father had dispatched a part of his books into the country, the rest were stored in the vestry room of the venerable and beloved St. John's Church. He never saw them again except a few volumes recaptured by our people..."

On the day following the march of the 1ˢᵗ Vermont Infantry into Hampton, Major Cary went to Fort Monroe to make a request of General Butler. He wanted to secure the release of three slaves, the property of Charles K. Mallory, who had escaped to Fort Monroe seeking sanctuary. General Butler refused the request on the grounds that Virginia was no longer part of the Union and could not expect to have the Fugitive Slave Law enforced. Moreover, he knew that slaves were being used to build fortifications and could therefore be considered "contraband of war". This action resulted ultimately in the movement of thousands of runaway slaves to Fort Monroe. Once there, the protected slaves were given employment by the Army. They constructed living quarters for themselves using whatever materials were available,

More Federal troops began to arrive on the Peninsula and some were encamped at Newport News. This opened Hampton to occupation by General Butler's troops. The military took over buildings that had been abandoned by their civilian owners. There were some fortifications constructed, including a ditch and embankment around St. John's Church.

General Butler determined in June to continue pressing the Confederates He counted on his numerical superiority to take more territory and to disrupt the southerners work on defensive positions. His advance led to the Battle of Big Bethel on June 10, 1861. It was the first battle of the Civil War and a victory for the Confederates who lost only one man killed, compared to eighteen for the Federals. Even though the results were miniscule compared to events that were to follow, the victory was greeted with much enthusiasm throughout the South.

The burning of Hampton, August 7, 1861.

Another event affecting the military forces in the vicinity of Hampton was the Southern victory at the first battle of Manassas on July 21, 1861. So great was the consternation in Washington at the defeat of Federal troops that fear grew for the security of Washington itself. As a result, General Butler was ordered to return 4,000 men from the Virginia Peninsula to the Washington area. With the drawdown of Federal troops, General Butler withdrew his military forces from Hampton. During the withdrawal one-third of the town was burned.[6]

All the conditions except one were now in place that led to the complete burning of Hampton, including the destruction of St. John's Church. Forces at Fort Monroe could reoccupy Hampton at any time. The town was deserted by its normal occupants and unoccupied by Federal troops; the flight of slaves to the "Freedom Fort" was underway and growing day by day. After the victory at Big Bethel, Confederate troops were emboldened to strike at Federal targets. All that was needed to precipitate the destruction of the town was for General Butler to make public his intention to use Hampton in the future for quartering of troops or contrabands.

After General Butler announced his intentions to occupy Hampton, they were published in the northern press. When a copy of this information fell into the hands of the Confederate commander, General Magruder, he decided to take advantage of the opportunity to strike. After finding that men in his command who lived in Hampton agreed with his plan, he determined to move ahead.

A force of four companies was assigned to the mission and moved into Hampton on the night of August 7, 1861. The Confederates left their horses by the wall of St. John's Church and moved to the center of town. Each of the four companies was assigned a quarter of the town to put to the torch. Some soldiers torched their own homes. The few remaining occupants had little time to escape with more than their lives. Union troops who witnessed from the east bank of the Hampton River recalled the sight,

> "The night was black and the wind blew freshly from the south. At about nine o'clock our pickets were suddenly startled by the shouting of the negroes (who still remained in the village), and presently the regular tramp of marching soldiers was heard by our men. Then appeared two long rows of torches, lighting up the dark, narrow ways and the windows of the deserted houses. Suddenly the column halted, and the flaming torches were seen dancing wildly in all directions, like so many will-o-the-wisps. And now the quiet of the night was broken by loud yells, the houses were entered and fired. And soon the whole town was enveloped in flames, casting a bright light over the bay, and revealing to our soldiers the forms of the enemy as they moved about the streets..."[7]

A Union correspondent wrote, describing the aftermath of the fire,

> "Nothing but a forest of bleak sided chimneys and walls of brick houses tottering and cooling in the wind, scorched and seared trees and heaps of smoldering ruins mark the site. A more desolate sight cannot be imagined than is Hampton today."[8]

Ruins of the church, 1861.

A chilling observation comes from the wartime diary of Jacob Heffelfinger, a Union soldier who later became a leading citizen of Hampton and a vestryman of St. John's Church,

> "Monday, 18 August 1862,
> Made a trip to the ground once occupied by the village of Hampton."

The damage to St. John's Church was described by Union topographer Robert Sneden,

> "Keeping through the town I came upon the ruins of St. John's Episcopal Church. The fire had gutted it completely. The tower had

fallen down all in a heap, roofs clean gone, and nothing but bare walls left standing. Not a piece of woodwork of any kind could be seen but a few ends of timbers sticking up out of piles of burnt bricks, some of the fine trees around the graveyard were scorched black and dead, others were in full leaf."[9]

Abraham Lincoln and some of his cabinet visited Fort Monroe in May, 1862, to meet with his military commanders. During his visit he determined to ride to Hampton to see the destroyed town. Secretary Stanton and others elected to ride in a carriage while President Lincoln and Treasury Secretary Salmon P. Chase chose to ride on horses. Secretary Chase later recorded the scene when they viewed the ruins of St. John's Church,

"...the old church amid the graves of generations, a gem of a building...where generation after generation of Virginians had been baptized, confirmed, married, admitted to the Communion, and dismissed with tears and benedictions to their last repose.

...We returned from Hampton saddened."[10]

The appearance of Hampton after the fire of August 7, 1861.

Eighteen

The Civil War

With the church and town destroyed and the congregation dispersed, it is not surprising to learn that the minister also left. The Reverend Jacobs went to Bloomfield parish in Rappahannock County where he was reported to be in service in 1862.[1] As for Hampton, it became little more than a staging area for troops as General McClellan began his campaign to march up the Virginia Peninsula to Richmond. On another visit to Hampton, Union topographer Robert Sneden writes,

> "March 25, 1862...The army marched through the town until late at night, large bonfires were made to light their way. The fire shone on the tall burnt chimneys, making quite a theatrical effect."

While Hampton was a scene of devastation, Fort Monroe continued to bustle with activity.

Sneden continues,

> "March 30,1862...Troops and stores are still being landed at wharves at Fortress Monroe. White tents cover the large fields in every direction.
> "April 1, 1862...Fine day. I walked to Fort Monroe and had oysters at the Hygeia Hotel. Met several of my old acquaintances whom I had not seen since leaving Alexandria. I walked the beach to the rear of the

fort and watched with my glass the fleet at anchor and the rebel batteries at Sewell's Point…"[2]

The migration of escaping slaves to Fort Monroe continued. In a census of freedmen, conducted by the Union army in 1863, a total of 9,500 black refugees were reported to be concentrated in the refugee camps of the lower peninsula. Many of these refugees, called contrabands, made homes for themselves on the site of burned out Hampton. The contrabands utilized the remaining standing chimneys where possible for their own houses.[3]

The policy of the Union Army was to provide employment to contrabands in the engineer and quartermaster departments of Fort Monroe. Lumber was also issued for the building of houses. In the summer of 1862, contrabands renovated the courthouse in Hampton for use as a church and school. In this effort they were assisted by missionaries of the American Missionary Association. Preferring self-employment, some refugees turned to fishing and harvesting oysters to make a living.[4]

For the members of the congregation of St. John's Church who had gone off to war, events of the conflict spread over a wide area. Three men – George Booker, Jacob Heffelfinger, and George Semple, who were members of the vestry after the war, had experiences that illustrate the intensity of the conflict

George Booker was the son of a prosperous farmer in Elizabeth City County. Before the war, he had been a student at Colonel Cary's Hampton Military Academy and enlisted at Hampton in the Confederate Army. He was severely wounded and captured by Union forces. According to family legend, he was cared for by an order of Roman Catholic nuns while he was still a prisoner. Before being paroled and returned to the South, he asked what he might do to thank the nuns for their kindness. They responded that if he later had daughters, he could send them to a convent school. The severity of his wound can be judged from the fact that three months later, after he was paroled, he was still hospitalized in Richmond where surgeons operated to remove pieces of bone that were causing him pain.

After the war, George Booker returned to Hampton. Like most of the local landowners, his father had lost almost everything during the Civil War. Young Booker married and had a family, including several daughters.

Drawing of occupied Hampton in 1862 shows
the ruins of the church in right background.

True to a commitment he made to the convent nuns, he sent his daughters to be educated at the Georgetown Visitation Convent in Washington, D.C. George Booker was in business and served as postmaster at Fort Monroe. He also was the owner of the Sherwood Inn, a hotel located at Old Point Comfort near the fort.[5]

Most of the men of St. John's Church were in the Confederate Army, with many in the 32nd Virginia Infantry, the unit that absorbed the militia of the Virginia Peninsula. Jacob Heffelfinger, however, was a Union soldier, a member of the 26th Pennsylvania Infantry. Considering the hardship of his service and the severity of his wounds, it is remarkable that Jacob Heffelfinger chose to live in Hampton after the war.

Heffelfinger's unit was a part of McClellan's Army that passed through Fort Monroe in order to participate in the Peninsula Campaign in 1862. He was wounded and captured in the Seven Days Battle and then again wounded and captured in the Battle of Fredericksburg. In the prison hospital at the end of 1862, he wrote in his diary,

"A year of bloody work for poor bleeding America, and how dark the future yet appears. God help us and save us in the involuntary expressions of our hearts."[6]

Dr. George W. Semple was a vestryman who had been practicing medicine in Hampton since 1846. He enlisted in the Confederate Army in Hampton and was appointed Surgeon of the 32nd Virginia Infantry in May, 1861. The next year he was placed in charge of General Hospital Number 21 in Richmond where he served until the end of the war.[7] His son, Edward A. Semple, enlisted in the Confederate Army at the age of nineteen, rose to the rank of major, and was captured shortly before the end of the war. Edward Semple began a career as a civil engineer after the war and later became the surveyor of Elizabeth City County.

Dr. George W. Semple,
Confederate Surgeon.

It is difficult to imagine the strains of warfare on the people who had been, or were to be, the congregation of St. John's Church. The southeastern area of the United States underwent great convulsions of fighting and occupation by opposing armies with much of the activity centered in Virginia. Men had little idea of what danger might face them from one day to the next. For their families it was perhaps even worse. Unaware of what was happening to the soldiers, their wives had serious problems of keeping the family together and even survival. For the people of Hampton, great losses occurred very early in the war with the burning of the town. The opposing armies hardly finished one battle before they began preparing for the next. There was continual naval activity in Hampton Roads, including the Battle of the *Monitor* and the *Merrimack*. The families that had once been happy here knew that Hampton, which had been their home, was to be in occupied territory until the end of the war.

George Ben West's family had owned a farm and also a house in Hampton on Queen Street opposite St. John's Church. His brother, while a Confederate soldier, had ignited the fire in the parlor of their house in Hampton. West later wrote about returning to town in 1865,

"What a change on the Peninsula!... The old St. John's Church walls remain standing and also the walls of the house of Mr. Kennon Whiting. The bridge across the creek had been rebuilt, and as I walked up the street I could not locate a single place, and when I reached the cross streets [King and Queen], I could hardly believe it was so near the foot of the bridge. The old St. John's Church was the only place I recognized."[8]

The grave of the Rev. Mark Chevers who died in 1875.

Part III

Recovery and Growth
1865 - 2008

Nineteen
Rebuilding Again

Ben West observed accurately that the life of farmers returning to the Virginia Peninsula was not an easy one. He later wrote about them,

> "…without a cent of money; their houses in most cases gone; their fields grown up in bushes; the ditches all filled; with no stock; most of them in debt, and property mortgaged; and a good deal of the property sold or in Federal courts to be sold for taxes."[1]

While West's observation pertained to families like his own who lost farms in Elizabeth City County, the situation for Hampton residents was just as bad, or perhaps worse. Those who had farms could at least cut trees for their firewood or to sell to others in order to raise money. Farm patterns were greatly changed because slaves no longer worked the land. The larger farms were broken up through sales or rental arrangements. But nothing had happened to change the fertility of the land and truck farming emerged as an important economic activity after the Civil War.

There was another means of livelihood available to the local population because of the waters that surrounded Hampton. The seafood industry provided an immediate return in either food for the table or for sale in the marketplace. Men harvested the fish, clams, oysters, crabs and other seafood using whatever boats were available. Adapted from Indian practices centuries earlier, pound nets were used for fishing.

Returning to Hampton after the Civil War, parishioners of St. John's could not worship in the church which had been so badly damaged, They met to worship under lay leadership at Patrick Henry Hall on nearby Court Street.[2] There is a picture of the frame building, which is no longer standing, in the museum of St. John's Church. The congregation rented the first floor and arranged it as a chapel with pews and lectern. Families that attended in 1869 were mostly members that had attended prior to the war such as Whiting, Booker, Semple, Mallory, Hope, and Sclater.

In June 1869, the Reverend John McCarty, who had retired as a United States Army chaplain, began his service as the minister of St. John's Church. He was uncompensated for his ministry which extended far beyond normal expectations. There was a congregation to be restored and a church to be rebuilt. Fund raising had begun in 1866, with the first contribution received from the clerk of the courts, William S. Howard, who was a Baptist. Persons from other denominations and from all over the country sent in contributions. Former rectors of St. John's church sent money collected from their congregations. Over $3,600, a considerable sum for the time, was raised for restoration of the church.

Francis M. Whittle, Assistant Bishop for the Diocese of Virginia, visited the restored church on April 13, 1870. At this time he confirmed ten persons. Bishop Whittle in his report to the Council said,

> "This grand old building, of which there was nothing left after the war, save the walls, by exertions of the people and the assistance of friends at a distance, has been so far restored as to be again used for the worship of God. Permanent seats and chancel furniture are still wanting. As no people in the Diocese have been more impoverished, and none have been more willing even beyond their power, to repair their own desolations, so none are more deserving of help than the people of Hampton."

Help for the struggling church also came from newcomers to Hampton. Among the newcomers was Jacob Heffelfinger, who, as a Union soldier, had previously been in Hampton during campaigns of the Civil War. For the rest of his life, he carried a memory of walking from the Union Army hospital, crossing the bridge on Queen Street, and reaching the ruins of the church. There he found his company mates bivouacked along the church walls.[3]

Heffelfinger returned to Hampton from Pennsylvania in 1866 and married Louisa Whiting of Hampton. He established a lumber company on waterfront property at the foot of King Street. With the passage of time, the business expanded to cover a wide range of building materials including mill work. It was the type of industry needed to support construction of a new town. Heffelfinger's Civil War diaries show that he never missed an opportunity to attend religious services. He showed the same devotion after the war when he joined the congregation of St. John's Church and participated in its rebuilding. For the remainder of his life Jacob Heffelfinger served St. John's with unmatched energy in positions of responsibility

In 1866, James S. Darling departed New York City for Hampton where he busied himself in several enterprises including a lumber mill and a fish oil plant. His most significant endeavor, however, was in the planting and packing of oysters. The firm of J.S. Darling and Son employed hundreds of workers and its mammoth pile of oyster shells became a Hampton landmark. Other enterprises he founded included a streetcar company and a beach hotel at Buckroe. His wife's name is recorded on the list of pew-holders at St. John's Church in 1872.

James McMenamin, a newcomer from Massachusetts, did for the crab industry what J.S. Darling did for oysters. He invented a canning process that enabled the shipment of crab meat without spoiling to distant markets. He likewise employed hundreds of workers.

A member of a family who had been missionaries in Hawaii, Samuel Armstrong had commanded a regiment of black soldiers during the Civil War. He was convinced that education was essential to the advancement of Americans who had formerly been enslaved. As an officer in the Freedmen's Bureau after the war, he recognized the potential for establishing a school at Hampton. With the assistance of the American Missionary Association, General Armstrong purchased a farm and in 1868 established the Hampton Normal and Agricultural Institute. By the 1880's, the school had grown to an enrollment of nearly a thousand.

Before the Civil War, Old Point Comfort was known for the Hygeia Hotel. The hotel did not survive the war; it was removed to improve the defenses of Fort Monroe. After the war, Harrison Phoebus, a native of Maryland, bought the new Hygeia Hotel and expanded it into a destination for travelers arriving by boat or train. It was a splendid hotel and offered the latest conveniences for its guests.[4]

These examples of viable industries, each having energetic leaders, help explain how a devastated community could recover relatively quickly after the Civil War. There was construction, the seafood industry, farming, Hampton Institute, and the Hygeia Hotel. All of these were engines for recovery and growth.

Even though the pre-war buildings were gone from Hampton, the streets remained. But, in addition, there were streets named Lincoln, Grant, and Union. Members of the black community built along these streets in the locale where newly freed slaves had settled during the Civil War. For two decades after the war, blacks were in the majority and enjoyed political power to elect city officials.

The Reverends John J. Norwood, William Jarrett, and J.W. Keeble served relatively briefly as ministers in the early and mid 1870s. Of longer duration was the appointment in 1876 of the Reverend John J. Gravatt, who served until 1893.

The Reverend Gravatt came to Hampton on the night boat from Washington to take up his new position at St. John's Church. He arrived on a cold rainy morning at Old Point Comfort and found a horse-drawn cab from a local livery stable to carry him the three miles to Hampton. The rains had turned the unpaved roads into a morass of mud. When the cab sank in the mud over its axles, he had little choice but to dismount and help his driver push. On rainy days it was still difficult for people outside the town to reach St. John's Church. But things were changing. It was the beginning of the era that would see paved roads, sidewalks that were illuminated at night, and electric street cars.[5]

This was also a period of growth for St. John's Church. The number of communicants grew from fifty-nine to two hundred and thirty-two during the ministry of Mr. Gravatt. Many physical replacements or additions, including a new organ, were made to meet the needs of the church.[6]

The rebuilding of the interior reflected the styles of the late nineteenth century. Thus a visitor today will find St. John's to have an exterior that is colonial but whose interior is that of the Victorian period. The rich hues of the opened timbered ceiling contrast to the white walls beneath. Sunlight playing on the stained glass windows provides beautiful images to the viewer.

The vestry undertook the building of a parish house in 1886. The project required four years for the acquisition of land, development of plans, and actual construction. This building provided additional space for Sunday school instruction and has been added to many times in the years since.

In 1879 St. John's Church welcomed its first eleven Indian communicants who had come from the Great Plains to be students at Hampton Institute. The number

The Reverend John J. Gravatt, Rector 1876-1893.

increased during the remainder of the nineteenth century. Mr. Gravatt himself recruited many of these Indians to come to study at Hampton. Students with names such as Solomon Yellow Hawk and Lucy Little Eagle, were among the forty-four Native American communicants in 1904. One of the most beautiful windows in the church depicts the baptism of Pocahontas. Bishop Whittle, a descendant of Pocahontas, suggested the creation of the window. It was the gift of Indian students and other friends who left a fitting memorial at the church that traces its history to the site of the Indian town of Kecoughtan.

The Parish House was completed in 1889.

Twenty

Time of Mission

The period following the Civil War was a time of change for the Diocese of Virginia. Membership in the churches grew rapidly, at a rate of growth larger than that of the Episcopal Church nationwide. Political changes during the war had an impact. Part of Virginia was severed to form the state of West Virginia. It is not surprising that the Diocese of West Virginia was formed in 1877 to conform to the new state boundaries.

A change that had a greater impact on St. John's Church was the creation of the Diocese of Southern Virginia in 1892. Churches of the new diocese now looked to Norfolk for leadership rather than to Richmond. Bishop Alfred M. Randolph, who had been assistant bishop to Bishop Whittle, was the first bishop of the Diocese of Southern Virginia.[1]

With the objective of establishing new congregations, the mission budget of the diocese supported the assignment of assistant rectors to established churches. In 1880, the Reverend Charles Mayo was assigned to St. John's Church as Assistant Rector for the purpose of renewing the Episcopal Church in Newport News. Eventually St. Paul's Church was established in 1883 and a church building was constructed in 1889.

Vestry minutes of St. John's Church show that in November, 1888 the vestry approved a request for three hundred dollars to support the work of an African American Episcopal Priest in Hampton. There is no record, however, of such a ministry taking place. But, there was interest growing in creating a church for African American Episcopalians. The Reverend

Gravatt was also working with students at Hampton Institute. Of the rector's annual salary of fifteen hundred dollars, two hundred was for this additional ministry.

Action began to create an Episcopal church in Phoebus, or "Chesapeake City" as it was then known. A Sunday school was organized by seven families in 1885. These families met in a rented hall over a grocery store until they grew enough to meet in a school. In 1887, St. John's Church established a mission church in Phoebus with the work of organization done by the Reverend Charles Mayo. Mr. Mayo and Mr. Gravatt would carry a portable organ in their horse drawn buggy when traveling to Phoebus to conduct services. In April, 1897, the cornerstone for Emmanuel Church was laid and the first service was conducted on July 4th of that year. In March of the following year Bishop Randolph was present for the confirmation of five candidates. Indian students at Hampton Institute made the furniture for the new church including the altar which is still in use today.[2]

The Reverend Gravatt resigned his position at St. John's Church in September, 1893, to answer the call of Holy Trinity Church in Richmond. St. John's had grown in numbers and materially under his leadership. Mission work led by him extended from Indian tribes in the west to students at Hampton Institute and new congregations on the Virginia Peninsula. John Gravatt is credited with "putting St. John's Church solidly back on its feet after the Civil War."[3]

The Reverend C. Braxton Bryan became the rector in November, 1893. His salary was fifteen hundred dollars annually as the Reverend Gravatt's had been, with two hundred dollars allocated for work at Hampton Institute. He was a man with a feisty personality and decided views. Although he was loved by his congregation, he had the habit of scolding them about once a year in a sermon. When someone asked the reason for his strong language, he replied,

> "Every year each vessel ought to be hauled up in dry dock and have its bottom scraped. People need the same treatment."[4]

The congregation must have loved the Reverend Bryan in return because the number of communicants grew from two hundred forty-nine in 1894 to four hundred ten in 1904.

Portable organ used for visits to mission churches.

During the ministry of Mr. Bryan, material improvements to St. John's Church included a new organ, vesting rooms for the choir in a tower added to the church, and chancel furniture. The most unique addition, however, was the Colonial Clergy window which was installed in 1903. This window in the north wall of the church depicts the arrival of the earliest English clergy. In addition to showing the names of the colonial clergy, the window bears the seal of the English missionary society, the Society for the Propagation of the Gospel in Foreign Parts.

A controversy arose when the proposal to create this window was first made by the donor, the Association for the Preservation of Virginia Antiquities, or APVA. The Reverend Bryan was not in favor of listing all the colonial clergy because this would honor the memory of the Reverend Jeremiah Taylor, who had been notorious for his misconduct. The APVA insisted on his inclusion, however, because he had without question been a minister here. Finally a compromise was reached: Taylor's name would be included on the window but it would be shown in brackets.

Colonial Clergy window.

In retrospect, the controversy increased our appreciation of the colonial ministers who did so much for the church in the seventeenth and eighteenth centuries. As the Reverend Reverdy Estill wrote,

> "The colonial clergy are shown to be, not monsters of vice, or seekers after worldly pleasure; they were, with rare exceptions, gentlemen, scholars, leaders of the people in righteousness, and living clean, upright lives themselves."

A group of young women in the church expressed a tolerant view of the Reverend Taylor when they created a social organization for charitable purposes that they called the Bracket Club.

In March of 1905, a group of Episcopalians in Newport News petitioned the vestry of St. John's Church to build a chapel in Newport News on 22nd Street. In April, Bishop Randolph approved the chapel. St. John's was to hold title to the 22nd Street property for Grace Church. The building committee reported that the church was completed in March, 1907.

In late 1904, the Reverend Bryan notified the vestry he intended to answer the call to be rector of Grace Church in Lynchburg, Virginia. The vestry appointed Jacob Heffelfinger head of a three man committee to seek a new rector. In April the committee recommended the Reverend Reverdy Estill, then rector of St. Paul's Church in Louisville, Kentucky. In early May, Dr. Estill met with the vestry and on May 16, 1905 he accepted their call to St. John's Church.

In calling Dr. Estill, St. John's Church had chosen a minister of unusual warmth and consideration for the feelings of others. He was known for treating every person, regardless of station, with courtesy and respect. Twice a widower and a veteran of the Civil War, he was no longer a young man when he took up his duties at St. John's Church. Nevertheless, he energetically entered into the life of the community.

E. Sclater Montague, who was later to become a well-known Hampton attorney and the Senior Warden of St. John's Church, wrote that at the age of ten years, he was not known for his good behavior in school. His parents and grandmother were so concerned they went to Dr. Estill for advice. Dr. Estill's reply was to the effect that the boy should be left alone

Dedication of the cross at the rediscovered site of the second church, 1914; from left: the Rev. C. Braxton Bryan, Mr. Jacob Heffelfinger, the Rev. Edwin R. Carter.

and maybe he would grow out of it. Montague wrote that he was always grateful for that advice to his elders.[5]

Like his predecessors, Mr. Gravatt and Mr. Bryan, the Reverend Estill supported members of the African American community interested in the formation of a mission church. A Sunday school for African Americans had been meeting as early as 1904 in the parish house of St. John's Church. There were seven teachers and sixty-eight students.[6] The Reverend Maximo P. Duty of Richmond visited Hampton and encouraged the group to form a congregation. In 1905, St. Cyprian's Church was begun. Dr. Estill conducted services for St. Cyprian's on Sunday afternoons or Thursday evenings. The congregation moved into its first building in 1907 at 136 Lincoln Street. Mr. Edward Spennie, one of the original members, made and donated the chancel furniture.[7]

Like St. John's, St. Cyprian's has occupied several sites in it church history. The second building, erected in 1963, was located near the campus of Hampton University on land leased from the school. The present church building was dedicated in June, 1984, and is located on West Queen Street.

At the same time that St. John's Church was looking forward in mission, a discovery was made that drew thoughts back to the early days of its existence. Jacob Heffelfinger reported to the vestry that he found the site of the second church on March 18, 1910. These were the foundations of the building that had fallen into disrepair and was torn down by court order in 1698. Memorial services were held at the site; and, in 1914, a monument in the form of a cross was erected by the Daughters of the American Revolution. The site was on the property of Mrs. Virginia Tabb who deeded the property to the church with the only condition that it be kept in order.[8] Today the site is protected by a wall erected in 1970 by the Kecoughtan Branch of the Association for the Preservation of Virginia Antiquities.

The Reverend Reverdy Estill, Rector 1905-1911.

The Reverend Reverdy Estill died suddenly on the morning of May 23, 1911. He had officiated at a funeral the day before and attended a meeting of the YMCA that evening. Only six years of his forty year ministry had been spent in Hampton, but he had come to be known by the entire community. Newspaper reports state that his funeral was attended by an estimated three thousand people. A procession led by Bishop Randolph and other clergymen walked from the rectory on King Street to Queen Street and then to the church. So that adults and children could see the procession, all the offices and schools of the town and county closed for the event. Out of deep respect for Dr. Estill, the businesses of Hampton, including the banks and even the saloons, were closed during the funeral. Crowds that could not be accommodated in the church gathered outside for the gravesite service. Seven Indian students from Hampton Institute were honorary pallbearers. St. Cyprian's Church held an additional memorial service. The Reverend E. H. Hamilton, Rector of St. Cyprian's, said that Dr. Estill had been more than a father and inspiration to him.[9] The altar of St. John's Church was dedicated to the memory of Dr. Estill.

In a span of less than two decades St. John's Church had helped to establish four churches: Emmanuel in Phoebus, St. Paul's in Newport News, Grace in Newport News, and St. Cyprian's in Hampton. It was truly a time of growth, unparalleled since colonial days.

St. Cyprian's Church was founded in 1905.

Twenty-One
Make a Joyful Noise

For many years, Calvinistic influences affected the quality of church music in Virginia. Even though in England there was an abundance of beautiful music from the Elizabethan period, music brought by early colonists was from the Geneva hymn book. The influence of low church practices extended to prohibiting the use of vestments or robes for choirs. Changes were made that ameliorated the severity of low church practices, but the changes were strongly resisted and consequently were very gradual.

On December 12, 1902 the *Newport News Press* reported that "the newly organized choir" of St. John's Church had held its first rehearsal on the previous evening. It went on to say that within six weeks a new organ was to be ready for service and that at that time the choir would make its first appearance in vestments. The vestments were especially ordered for the choir from London. For its first appearance as a vested choir, the choir would open the service by processing. The newspaper reported this was to be the first service of a church in Hampton where a choir processed.

In a diocese long accustomed to low church practices, the participation of a vested choir was an innovation. St. John's appears to have made the transformation irreversibly; its choirs ever since have worn robes. There is a photograph from circa 1902 that shows vestments being worn by Indian singers from Hampton Institute who were organized as an Indian choir at St. John's Church.[1]

St. John's Indian choir, 1902,
with the Rev. Bryan.

Extending from at least 1853, the use of organs in providing church music was a welcomed addition. The new organ installed in 1903 was located on the first floor of the recently completed church tower. The pipes were located on the north side of the chancel where the chapel is located today. For the next seventy-five years the organ was located at the front of the church and the choir pews were located in the chancel.

The Reverend Edwin R. Carter, who became rector in 1912, took an active interest in the choir. He had a fine singing voice. It was Mr. Carter's practice to sing the psalms, and, about once a month, he sang an offertory solo.[2] He had the choir formally organized as a guild with himself as ex-officio president and the choir director as vice president. There were a number of committees including a membership committee who were to seek out persons who would make good additions to the choir. All singers would then be voted on for choir membership. Despite the formal sounding arrangement, the choir was enjoyed by its members as a social as well as a service organization. Once each month it held its weekly rehearsal at the home of a member to conduct choir business as well as to rehearse. Rehearsals ended with the serving of refreshments.

Miss Nancy Jones was a lay person who, in the role of Sunday school teacher, exerted a lasting influence over a group of young people who attended St. John's Church. In about 1912 she was teaching a class of twelve high school boys when she suggested that they ask a group of girls from the Sunday school to join them. This was the beginning of a Sunday school class that became known as the Knights and Ladies. With Miss Nancy and other church members as chaperons, they met for parties at the homes of the members as well as for occasional dances. Over a period of four decades young people attending the Sunday school became Knights or Ladies. In appreciation of her loving guidance, her former students dedicated a stained glass window in the church to Miss Nancy Jones.

Jacob Heffelfinger was another lay person whose devotion to the people of St. John's Church extended over a period of decades. As mentioned earlier, he settled in Hampton shortly after the Civil War and became a member of St. John's Church. For nearly three decades Heffelfinger served as vestryman, treasurer, and superintendent of the Sunday school. Vestry books of the period are filled with the detailed entries he made for the church accounts. These accounts include expenditures for the many improvements he supported such as enlargement of the parish house in 1910.[3] If a Christian can be identified by service to the body of Christ, Jacob Heffelfinger was indeed a Christian.

There is a legend that illustrates his desire to play a leading role in church matters. It seems that the vestry decided to replace the bell in the parish house tower. Jacob Heffelfinger did not concur in this expenditure and voted against it. When the new bell arrived by steamboat at Old Point Comfort, however, he had a change of heart. He immediately proceeded to the dock, had the bell loaded on his wagon and returned to Hampton. He then proudly led the wagon carrying the bell down Queen Street to St. John's Church.

The bell that has rung so sweetly for weddings and solemnly for funerals, as well as summoning the faithful to worship, has also given the alarm for the volunteer firefighters of Hampton. The volunteer fire department became active after a disastrous fire in 1884 that destroyed thirty-three buildings in the town. The number of peals, from one to four, indicated that the fire was in one of four quadrants formed by the intersection of King and Queen Streets. Only recently removed from the tower, a sign listing the number of peals and their meaning also carried the warning to overactive boys that anyone meddling with the bell was subject to a fine of $5.00.

The Reverend Carter exercised a very positive influence over the younger members of the congregation. As a result of his encouragement and example several young men indicated an interest in entering the ministry. John Boyd Bentley was one of these but his education was interrupted by military service. The local National Guard unit, Battery D of the 1st Virginia Field Artillery, was called to active duty on the Mexican Border in June of 1916.[4] Bentley was one of the young men of Hampton

National color and service flag displayed during World War I.

in Battery D. This was followed by service in World War I. (Nine of Nancy Jones' original twelve Knights served in World War I as did seventy-five other men from the parish). After the War, Bentley attended the College of William and Mary and the Virginia Theological Seminary. He began service as a clergyman in Alaska in 1921.

Samuel H. Sayre was another young man whom the Reverend Carter encouraged toward a vocation in the ministry. Sayre attended the Virginia Theological Seminary and later became the Dean of the National Cathedral in Washington.

In 1922 the Reverend Charles E. McAlister succeeded Mr. Carter as the rector of St. John's Church. He is said to have "preached an excellent sermon" and often filled the church to capacity. A parishioner, Dr. Harry D. Howe, is reported to have said that a visit by the Reverend McAlister to the sick room would do as much good as the visit of a doctor of medicine.[5]

In 1927 the Reverend George O. Watts became the new rector. He was a tall, likeable man with the mannerisms and speech which reminded people of Abraham Lincoln. Unfortunately, he was responsible for the tragic death of a pedestrian in an automobile accident in 1930. The car

Watts was driving skidded across the streetcar tracks and onto the sidewalk where it struck a young boy. The Reverend Watts died within about a year after the accident and is buried in the cemetery of St. John's Church.[6]

The all-male vestries of the early twentieth century were similar to those in colonial times in composition. They were generally leading citizens of the town, men who could get things done because of their affluence or influence, as well as their desire to serve. Frank W. Darling and Howard W. Saunders are examples. Darling's service on the vestry began in 1894 and extended to his death forty-seven years later. Darling's many civic activities included leadership of the volunteer fire department. He died while chairing a meeting of the Board of Directors of Hampton Institute. Howard W. Saunders, a native of Virginia, was the co-founder of a prominent insurance firm. He was a leader of the Sunday school as well as a member of the vestry. His grandson, Howard W. Saunders III, attended St. John's Church and graduated from Virginia Theological Seminary. He ministered at Emmanuel Church in Hampton and St. Andrews Church in Newport News.

Mrs. Frank W. Darling came to Hampton Institute from Vermont to be a teacher of Indian students. She was accustomed to attending St. John's Church with her Indian students. She went to Montana in 1891 to teach Native American children at the Fort Belknap Reservation and had a lifelong interest in Indian culture. Mollie Darling, as she was known to generations of Hamptonians, taught a Bible class at St. John's for over forty years. She and her husband Frank supported many church activities and hosted the town's Easter sunrise services and egg hunts on the lawn of "Cedar Hall", their home in Hampton. During World War I and World War II she encouraged servicemen to come to picnics at "Cedar Hall".

Mollie Darling also was the Diocesan President of the Episcopal Church Women from 1920 to 1924. She followed the precedent of women who for generations have taught in the Sunday schools, supported the guilds, and participated in mission work. She remained a member of the ECW Board and hosted many events until her death in 1955.[7]

E. Sclater Montague, who later became Senior Warden at St. John's Church, wrote of her,

> "The St. John's bible class was undoubtedly Mrs. Darling's chief

interest. She taught this class for approximately half a century, but I do not recall any organization or movement in Hampton to which she did not contribute."[8]

She provided the following resolutions for her class in the *Bible Class Bulletin* at the beginning of 1927,

NEW YEAR'S RESOLUTIONS
A Banner Class every Sunday,
A vital truth realized every Sunday,
A part taken in the week-day work of the church every week,
A welcome to the stranger in our midst at all times,
And happiness in our hearts every minute, even though things
do go dead wrong; and other lives made happy just because of
the members of St. John's Bible Class,
A Merry Christmas to all, my dears, God bless us every one.

Faithfully Yours,

Mary Gorton Darling

Twenty-Two

Swing Low, Sweet Chariot

The Reverend Theodore S. Will became rector of St. John's Church in 1932 and served until 1938. During this time he wrote a book entitled *The Episcopal Church*. Even though its scope extends from the introduction of Christianity into England to the American revolution and beyond, Will's book is remarkable for its profundity and brevity. It also covers the teachings of the church, including the meaning of the sacraments.[1] In addition to his scholarly attainments, Mr. Will was an able preacher. Unfortunately, in the later years of his tenure, Mr. Will did not enjoy the support of the entire vestry; they refused to support his efforts to become Bishop of the Diocese of Southern Virginia. Shortly after, he accepted a call to another church.[2]

Hampton's John B. Bentley who had gone to Alaska as a clergyman in 1921, returned to Virginia in 1926 as assistant rector of Bruton Parish Church in Williamsburg. It was the rector of Bruton Parish Church, the Reverend W.A.R. Goodwin, who made the recommendation to John D. Rockefeller to proceed with the restoration of colonial Williamsburg, a map was needed showing the town as it appeared in the 18th century. Fortunately, there was a map in the Library of the College of William and Mary that was drawn following the Battle of Yorktown by an engineer of the French Army. John Bentley was able to overcome the reluctance of the William and Mary Librarian Earl G. Swem to allow him to copy the topographic detail of the map needed for the restoration. The Frenchman's map helped to accurately identify foundations or locate buildings such as the Wythe house that were known to be in Williamsburg at the time.[3]

In 1931, John Bentley was consecrated as Suffragan Bishop of Alaska. During the next fifteen years he served in Alaska. Appeals were made to Sunday school children all over the country to support the missions in Alaska visited by Bishop Bentley. Most often Bishop Bentley's visits were made by means of dog sled. Children at St. John's Church enthusiastically raised money to buy food for Bentley's dogs. After a distinguished career in worldwide missions of the

The Reverend John B. Bentley, later Bishop of Alaska.

Episcopal Church, Bishop Bentley retired in 1965 to his native Hampton. Beginning a second career, John Bentley served the Diocese of Southern Virginia by travelling to various churches where he confirmed more than five thousand people.[4] He also found time to compile a book consisting of the gravestone inscriptions for the cemetery of St. John's Church.[5] Bentley's book has been a valuable asset in identifying old gravestones.

Born a slave on the eastern shore of Virginia, Solomon Fosque was employed at St. John's Church for thirty-six years. During the first twenty-four years of his service at St. John's Church, Solomon Fosque was the caretaker of the cemetery. In addition to keeping the churchyard beautiful, he took an active interest in the many gravestones in the cemetery and acted as guide to the visitors who came to see it.[6]

For the twelve years before his death in March, 1936, Solomon Fosque was the sexton of the church. He had also become a member of the church and was buried in the cemetery after a service conducted at St. John's. Vestry members served as his honorary pallbearers. The active pallbearers were chosen from the Elks lodge to which "Uncle Solomon" belonged.[7]

The graves of Willis Wilson (on left) and Dr. George Balfour.

The crosses on the roof of St. John's Church were donated by Solomon Fosque and are a memorial to him. His service is also commemorated on a bronze plaque in the west vestibule of the church. Fosque's grave is in the cemetery that he cared for during so many years.

The cemetery had begun even before the construction of the church in colonial times. During most of its history it was the town cemetery, not just the cemetery for St. John's Episcopal Church. 1701 was the date of the earliest known internment, the burial of Captain Willis Wilson whose family had owned the fifty acres on which the town of Hampton was built. Willis Wilson probably gave an acre and a half for the church and cemetery. The original gravestone was destroyed in the Civil War but the grave can still be found near the exterior east wall of the church.

Since the date of its construction in 1728, many of the rectors of St. John's Church have chosen to be buried in its cemetery. From colonial times until the present day, rectors, out of love for St. John's Church, have chosen to have their graves here. Most are buried close to the church

Grave of Hannah Tunnel who alerted the Confederates at Big Bethel.

Gravestone with inscription "November 31".

they served. Because of its age, the cemetery reflects the changing styles of gravestones. Among the oldest are stones with lengthy epitaphs and in the Victorian period symbols were used to express remembrance of young children or persons who died in the prime of life.

Dated April 11, 1798, Captain Henry Mowat's tombstone is near the walkway leading from Queen Street to the south door of the church. The inscription on the stone slab refers to Mowat's service in the British Navy. No mention was made of his burning the city of Portland, Maine in the Revolutionary War because the citizens refused to provision his ships. The words, "lamented universally" on the stone were probably an exaggeration. On the other side of the walkway one finds the Jennings tombstone bearing the erroneous date "November 31st".

Near the east wall of the church is the tombstone of Doctor George Balfour, who died in 1830. The stone bears twenty lines of inscription that relate his medical career, including Army service with General Anthony Wayne, the Revolutionary War hero, who died in Doctor Balfour's arms. Also there is an eight line self-written epitaph. Mingled with his remains are those of his parents who occupied the one hundred acres of land known

A portion of St. John's cemetery that extends north toward Lincoln Street.

as "Little England" near the town. James Balfour directed a mercantile operation there in the eighteenth century. With their son George, James and Mary Balfour were communicants at St. John's Church.[8] Portraits of the Balfours and their young son George are in the museum of the Virginia Historical Society in Richmond.

Near the Franklin Street entrance is the grave of Hannah Nicholson Tunnel. Prior to the Battle of Big Bethel in 1861, the first pitched land battle in the Civil War, Hannah Tunnel risked her life to warn the Confederate forces of the approach of Union troops.

Dr. George W. Semple returned to Hampton after the Civil War and continued his interrupted service on the vestry of St. John's Church. He was chosen to be President of the Virginia Medical Society in 1881 and served until his death in 1883. His grave, located near the walk by the north side of the church, bears the epitaph "The Beloved Physician". Dr. Semple was one of 147 Confederate veterans whose graves lie within the walls of the Cemetery. In addition to their individual monuments their graves can be distinguished by the plain Maltese crosses placed by the United Daughters of the Confederacy. More prominent is the statue of the Confederate soldier standing at parade rest and facing Queen Street. Near the center of old Hampton, the cemetery has grown larger with the passing years until it now occupies six acres comprising a park like setting of peace and calm.

The Hampton Roads and Huntington Garden Clubs have been very supportive of the cemetery of St. John's Church. In 1999 they contributed a landscape master plan of the cemetery. Subsequently, as a step toward implementing the plan, they provided a major planting of crepe myrtle trees along the main axis of the cemetery.

The cemetery's growth over the centuries has evolved in a pleasing symmetry. There is a single axis from the entrance walkway off Queen Street that extends through the church. From the north door, this axis continues to Lincoln Street. On either side of the axis are a series of family plots, many of which are set off by iron fences or low curbs. Beautiful dogwood and crepe myrtle trees complement the shrubbery. The resulting experience for the viewer is that of "being in a rare garden."[9]

Twenty-Three

To Be a Light

The Reverend Carter H. Harrison answered the call to serve at St. John's Church in 1938.

When he came, the town of Hampton was gripped in the economic depression that extended through the nineteen-thirties. Fortunately, Hampton could rely on the seafood industry and the Newport News Shipbuilding and Drydock Company was close enough to reach by streetcar. The nineteen-thirties also saw an increase in activity at nearby Langley Field where NACA, the predecessor of NASA, was employing engineers to expand the nation's knowledge of aeronautical engineering. Many of these engineers and their families made St. John's Church their spiritual home. Some, like William D. Mace, became members of the vestry while his wife Betty managed the cemetery.

Hampton's population was swelled in World War II by the influx of personnel to Fort Monroe, Fort Eustis and Langley Field. The threat of the enemy was apparent to residents of Tidewater Virginia who could observe burning ships torpedoed off the Atlantic coast. Residents also saw oil from those ships that washed up on Buckroe and Grandview beaches. Antiaircraft batteries were deployed to protect the shipyard and served as a visible reminder that the war was a serious matter. Men and women who came to work in the shipyard and the port had to be housed, but there was little excess housing available. Families opened their homes to boarders; and, construction resources that could be spared from the war effort were used sparingly to provide new housing. Mollie and Frank Darling again hosted Sunday picnics for servicemen at their home, "Cedar Hall". Neighbors of the Darlings contributed sugar or ham obtained with precious rationing stamps to the picnics. Once again, singing was a popular entertainment, although Mollie Darling said the soldiers did not sing as well as they had during World War I. Altogether, one hundred seventy men and women of the congregation served in the military, with seven giving their lives in defense of the nation.

The Reverend Carter H. Harrison, Rector 1938-1959.

The Reverend Carter Harrison was an appealing leader. When he entered a room, his presence was felt immediately. At a party, if a waltz were playing he would ask a young lady to dance. His Lenten sermons might be on topics like the wives of King Henry VIII, not necessarily spiritual but interesting. Young men would be invited to his cabin in the woods where they could see his collection of firearms and try their hand at shooting. Two young boys who had been troublesome to their Sunday school teacher were invited to his cabin where an appeal was made for their cooperation. One was Frank A. Edgar, Sr. who later became Senior Warden of St. John's Church; the other was C. Cabell Tennis who later became Bishop of Delaware. During Carter Harrison's years at St. John's a major addition was made to the parish house in order to accommodate more Sunday school students. The north balcony was added in the church in memory of Mollie Darling.

A sense of the Reverend Harrison's good will toward men can be gained from his reaction to civil rights activity in the 1950s. During this time rumors were spreading that black activists would appear at the Sunday services and possibly disrupt them by asking to be seated. When the ushers asked him what they should do in such an eventuality, he replied in a letter

Mr. Howard W. Saunders with Sunday school students,
gathered for the flowering of the cross, Easter 1938.

of instructions that anyone coming to the church would be welcomed and seated without question.

The Reverend Carter Harrison completed his service at St. John's Church in 1959 after a span of 21 years. He and his wife Margaret were loved by the congregation. Their home in the rectory on Victoria Boulevard where they raised four sons was always a scene of happy activity. Harrison later served as Rector of Hickory Neck Church in Toano.

During Mr. Harrison's ministry, the organist was John W. Starnes who served a total of thirty-nine years, beginning in 1919. Mr. Starnes was the respected teacher of music in the Hampton public schools. The choir was located in the chancel during this period with the organ nearby. Upon the retirement of Mr. Starnes in 1957, Harold Chapman became the organist. Chapman composed several musical works including *Crosses of Tears,* a musical cantata, and a score for *The Common Glory.* He was also director of the Peninsula Youth Orchestra and music director of the Peninsula Opera Society.[1]

William Parker came to work at St. John's Church in 1932 when he was a young boy. He remembers vividly his earliest tasks which included helping to dig graves in the cemetery. One evening he was busy finishing a grave. The other workers departed, not realizing William was still digging. When he finished it was dark and there was no one to help him out of the hole. His cries for help, however, were answered by guards at the jail nearby who saved him from spending the night in the cemetery. Undaunted, William Parker continued to work in the cemetery until he was chosen to be sexton, a post he has filled without ceasing except for World War II military service.

Mrs. Lavinia Stallings of St. John's Altar Guild with 1618 communion silver, about 1955.

The Reverend Francis W. Hayes, Jr., answered the call to become Rector of St. John's Church in September, 1960. He was a graduate of the University of Texas and the Virginia Theological Seminary who had served as rector of churches in Texas, Virginia, and Maryland. He is remembered for his supportive and encouraging manner toward his parishioners.

St. John's Church had grown during the postwar years; there were 1,030 communicants in 1960. But there were difficult times ahead. There was confusion and doubt about the direction in which the national church was leading. He understood the need for calm assurance of God's love during times of difficulty. The Reverend Hayes' maintenance of relationships with the Diocese of Southern Virginia helped to increase understanding. He served terms on the Executive Board and the Standing Committee of the Diocese and chaired the Department of Mission.

St. Mark's Church in Hampton was established as a mission church of St. John's in 1963. The Reverend Winston Hope, who had been an

assistant rector to Frank Hayes, was
the first rector of St. Mark's where
he served for nineteen years.[2] St.
Mark's was the fifth church on the
Virginia Peninsula that received
mission support from St. John's
Church.

In 1962, Hampton, Elizabeth
City County, and the town of
Phoebus, three separate political
entities, were consolidated as the
City of Hampton. This marked the
passing of one of the four original
counties of colonial Virginia, a
county whose boundaries had been
the original boundary of Elizabeth
City Parish. The single church of
Elizabeth City Parish was a distant

The Reverend Francis W. Hayes, Jr.,
Rector 1960-1979.

memory in Hampton which in 1962 had over one hundred churches
and synagogues of varying denominations. Elizabeth City Parish lives on,
however, as the name of the parish of St. John's Church.

St. John's has resisted the temptation to become solely an "historic
church". Living in the past rather than the present has been avoided.
Learning from the past, however, is a necessity to ensure the future of a
church. A store of knowledge was added to the history of St. John's Church
when the Association for the Preservation of Virginia Antiquities made
archeological explorations at the second site of the church. The report
by Eleanor S. Holt on the many artifacts uncovered and the subsequent
analysis help us to comprehend the worship of God as practiced by the
settlers during the early and middle decades of the seventeenth century.[3]
These artifacts were mounted and displayed in a small museum at St.
John's church largely through the efforts of Beverly Gundry, the parish
historian. Much of what has been preserved of St. John's history is the
result of her work.

The Reverend Hayes made a report to the vestry in 1970 when he had
completed ten years as rector. In his report he pointed out that in the early

days of the church, it was possible to move its location, as it had done three times, to serve the needs of the population. In the midst of urban redevelopment in 1970, however, it was no longer in a position to relocate, "even if it wanted to". The large cemetery and historic church building made moving impossible. He noted that church attendance had declined, although still averaging over four hundred worshippers each Sunday in the church. He therefore urged the vestry to a recommitment to maintain the attractiveness of the facilities, to show a concern for the spiritual and historic values of the church, and above all to enhance the programs of the church so that young families would travel the extra miles necessary to reach St. John's Church from outlying areas of the community.[4]

Mrs. Margaret Thornton became a member of the vestry in January, 1971. She was the first woman to serve on the vestry of St. John's Church. Since then, many more women have served on the vestry and its composition has come to more evenly reflect the membership of the congregation. Several women have followed the precedent set by Margaret Thornton when she was elected senior warden,

The Reverend Francis Hayes devoted his energies and skills as a teacher, builder, and leader of St. John's Church until his retirement in 1979. There is a stone bench and pavement marker located near the west entrance of the church that the congregation dedicated in memory of his leadership.

Twenty-Four

Feed My Sheep

In 1980, the Reverend Rodney L. Caulkins answered the call to become the Rector of St. John's Church. He was a graduate of the Virginia Theological Seminary and had served for eleven years as Rector of St. Margaret's Church in Woodbridge, Virginia. Rodney Caulkins was an especially articulate and forceful speaker. He stressed the importance of outreach on the part of St. John's. He set a goal of twenty-five percent of the operating budget going to purposes beyond the parish. Most of this amount was for the diocese but there were other recipients. Marion O. McKinney, the senior warden, was likewise a strong proponent of outreach. He was instrumental in establishing the Charitable Trust, the income from which was devoted to charitable purposes. McKinney, along with other men and women in the parish were strong supporters of Youth Challenge, a faith based ministry in Newport News that provides help to victims of addiction. When Youth Challenge was creating its dormitory for young women from a donated building, volunteers from St. John's worked to make the rooms livable and attractive. Similarly, when Youth Challenge undertook to renovate the former Peninsula Catholic High School into a home for young men, volunteers created a "St. John's wing" from what had been classroom space in the high school.

The Reverend Caulkins encouraged participation in other outreach programs including providing a week's shelter for the homeless, Thanksgiving and Christmas baskets for needy families, making sandwiches for weekend lunches for the elderly and children, and a food pantry for the needy.

In 1984, St. John's Church had the opportunity to sponsor a family of Cambodian refugees. After suffering imprisonment and the death of her husband, Mrs. Sot Ben and her family escaped the "killing fields" of the Khmer Rouge. Rodney Caulkins encouraged the family to come to Hampton. Members of St. John's Church volunteered to become sponsors for the Cambodians. The family consisted of three adults and five children ranging in age from

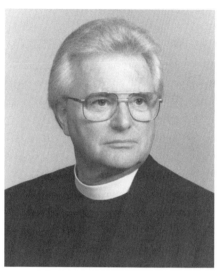

The Reverend Rodney L. Caulkins, Rector 1980-1999.

pre-school to middle school. Volunteers from St. John's Church helped the family find a place to live and places of employment for the three adults. On Sundays, the Cambodians attended Sunday school where they improved their English speaking skills. Today, all five of the children have grown to adulthood, graduated from college or apprentice schools, found employment in meaningful career fields, and started families of their own. They have shared their many happy moments with us and we have grieved with them over the death of one of the grandchildren who is buried in the cemetery of St. John's church.

In 1990, John Siderius became the organist and choir director. At the same time the Reverend Donna-Mae Siderius became the Assistant Rector of St. John's Church. Born and educated in Canada, she had graduated from McGill University and the Seminary at McGill. She was the first female clergy to serve at St. John's Church. She and her husband John were also the first husband and wife team employed by the church.

Before the Reverend Caulkins arrived at St. John's the organ had fallen into disrepair and action had been taken to install a replacement in keeping with the 1728 design of the church. The organ was relocated to a new gallery at the west end of the nave in cases that were designed

Organ of St. John's Church.

and built by Ralph Blakely. Unfortunately, defects in the new organ made it increasingly difficult to operate. It became necessary in 1993 to install another instrument designed by the Parsons Pipe Organ Builders. They worked with organist John Siderius to maintain the visual effect of an 18th century style and to create the outstanding tracker organ in use today.

John Siderius has continued the musical traditions of the church and also opened the doors of the church to those in the community who would enjoy the music. Periodic concerts by distinguished organists or singers and choral evensongs by the choir have provided opportunities for everyone to hear a rich range of music. He has directed two choirs for young people in which young singers have gained valuable experience while gaining knowledge of their musical heritage. He has given the adult choir the opportunity to expand its musical horizon by combining with the Bruton Parish choir and string orchestra to perform works such as Mozart's Coronation Mass.

Rodney Caulkins had a robust singing voice and theatrical ability. When the choir produced a musical play based on the adventures of Captain John Smith, the logical person to portray the role of John Smith was Rodney Caulkins. He had no difficulty adapting to the role of the bold British soldier who was an emissary to Chief Powhatan.

The Reverend Caulkins retired in April, 1999 after completing nineteen years as rector of St. John's Church. The Reverend Keith Adams accepted the call to be rector in October 2001 but resigned in May of the following year.[1] The vestry then called the Very Reverend Donna-Mae Siderius, who was at that time serving as Canon of the Ordinary of the Diocese of Southern Virginia.[2] She was installed as the forty-seventh rector of St. John's Church in January, 2003. Previously she had the distinction of being the first female clergy at St. John's Church. Now she was the first female rector.

The 1960s and 70s began a long period of challenge for Episcopal congregations. There was revision of the Book of Common Prayer, revision of the hymnal, and the ordination of women. But there was more to come. The election in 2003 of an openly homosexual priest to the position of Bishop of New Hampshire created a crisis in the Episcopal Church. Relations were disrupted within the church at the national, diocesan, and the parish level. Tensions were created that have not lessened with the

Acolytes in 1993
1st row from left: Ben Card, Grey Ligon, Chip Edwards, Chris Brauer, Beth Heath, Harper Lewis, Caitlyn Foster, 2nd row: Scott Gitchell, Harrol Brauer IV, McLean Favre, Meghan Foster, Katie Edwards, Stephen Price, Scott Curtis; 3rd row: Guy Neal.

passage of time as some dioceses and parishes have sought to separate themselves from the national church. Individuals objecting to the direction in which the national church appears to be headed have likewise separated themselves with a corresponding decrease in church membership. St. John's Church has not been an exception to this disaffection on the part of some individuals and families. The trend toward a declining church membership at St. John's Church, in part due to demographic factors, has not been reversed. In 2008 the number of communicants was 487.[3]

With the Reverend Donna-Mae Siderius' able leadership, St. John's Church has continued to enthusiastically support programs of outreach and mission. While continuing to participate in A Night's Welcome, the shelter and feeding program that is conducted during cold weather, St. John's also began a program of lunches on Wednesdays during the summer months. Open to anyone in the interest of fellowship, these free lunches show the church's concern for people living and working in the immediate vicinity as well as for church members. Financial support from St. John's Church has continued for diocesan projects such as Camp Chanco, as

The Very Reverend Donna-Mae Sidrius.

well as Jackson-Feild Home that St. John's has traditionally supported. Mission activities include pastoral visits to the women inmates at the city jail. There have been trips to areas of Louisiana and Mississippi struck by the devastating hurricane Katrina in 2005. St. John's Church members worked to rebuild destroyed homes. There have been mission trips for both adults and youths to Belize, the companion diocese in Central America, where parishioners worked on construction of a school. A strong youth program entitled Journey to Adulthood has included education and service by young people both within and outside the parish. Fund raising projects to support their mission trips have been an important element of youth activities. Donna-Mae Siderius has been an enthusiastic participant in the mission trips.

2002 marked the 70th year of service to St. John's Church by Sexton William Parker. His service was interrupted only by two years in the United States Army during World War II. If any trait characterized William Parker, it has been his sense of responsibility for the buildings and grounds of the church. He has been especially diligent less any harm come to his beloved St. John's. On his 70th anniversary, a cross dedicated to the memory of the service of William Parker was placed on the bell tower of the parish hall. His 76th anniversary was recognized in 2008.

In 2003, St. John's began a renovation of its parish house that had been constructed in increments over the period from 1889 to 1950. Known deficiencies were the kitchen that was inadequate for feeding large

2006 mission trip to aid Katrina victims in Mississippi.
From left: Whit McKinney, Sally Nisler, Debbie Williams, Kay Olson,
Frank Edgar, the Rev. David Copley, Dave Foster, Bob Harper.

groups and the flooring that had been repaired in patchwork fashion over the years. Unknown at the beginning of renovation was the amount of termite damage that the floors and vertical supports had suffered over the years. Floor joists had to be replaced under the main rooms and bearing columns at the ends of the stage were in danger of collapse. Fortunately, the expertise of the W.M. Jordan Construction Company and the dedication of Junior Warden William Terrill were available to save the parish house from condemnation. Hard work beautifully restored the crumbling building which then incorporated a more adequate kitchen. Financial support for the work was made possible through a bequest of

Sexton William Parker at the ceremony in 2002 to recognize his 70 years of service.

Mrs. Mary Williams. Patience and determination marked the efforts of the Reverend Donna-Mae Siderius and the church staff to keep church programs going during this challenging period.

With the major efforts on the parish house completed, The Reverend Siderius has now formed a committee to develop a plan for the renovation of the sanctuary of St. John's Church This plan respects its historic past and meets the needs of the worshipping community. The committee finds inspiration in the durability of the remarkable building that has served so well since 1728 and will continue to serve the parish after it begins its fifth century of existence in 2010.

Twenty-Five
A Fifth Century

As it begins its fifth century of parish life in 2010, St. John's Church finds strength and courage in the wonderful words and liturgy that characterize Episcopal worship. The distractions of the present time are certainly no greater than those faced by the early worshippers at colonial Kecoughtan who encountered starvation and disease, nor the difficulties experienced by the Anglican church when stripped of its prerogatives and property at the time of the American Revolution, nor the dismay in Hampton when the town was overrun by invaders in 1813, nor the anguish of those who fled their homes at the outbreak of the Civil War and returned to find those homes in ruins. Despite starvation and disease, the struggling colonists survived; confiscation of property destroyed some but not all of the Anglican churches; indignities suffered at the hands of foreign invaders strengthened the will of Americans to be independent; and the recovery from the Civil War, although long and costly, showed how friends and former enemies could unite in Hampton to rebuild and even help to establish new mission churches on the Virginia Peninsula.

There are only three buildings in present day Hampton that were existing in the eighteenth century. St. John's Church is one of them and the only one that is in the proximity of the town that the colonial government ordered to be built. Its significance in Hampton history is enhanced by being the established church at four successive sites from 1610 until 1776 and because for so long its cemetery has been used for

Altar of St. John's Church.

persons of all denominations.

Science and industry have increased our comforts and extended our life spans but men and women have not lost their need to look for spiritual support outside themselves. The church offers that support in prayers, praise, and instruction. The church also offers opportunities for service to others in a variety of ways, all of which enable the individual or family to bridge the gap between self and others.

There is a sanctuary in Hampton surrounded by a verdant cemetery where uncounted numbers of the departed rest in peace. The worshipers who congregate there cannot claim any exclusive right to the joy experienced by Christian people. They gather to worship their creator and hear the words of Holy Scripture that have endured through millenia past. They are willing to share the power of those words. The beauty of music offers them further inspiration. It is a place where the young can absorb the wisdom of the past and become prepared for the challenges and temptations that await them. It is a place of healing and solace and thanksgiving for the grace of God. That sanctuary is St. John's Church.

*At left, Harper Lewis with Sunday school
before egg hunt in the cemetery, Easter 2008.*

Appendix I

Ministers of Elizabeth City Parish, Hampton, Virginia and Their Years of Ministry

The Seventeenth Century

William Mays, 1610 – 1620
George Keith, 1621
Thomas White, 1622 – 1624
Jonas Stockton, 1624 – 1627
Rowland Graeme, 1628
William Wilkinson, 1635 – 1644

Justinian Alymer, 1645 – 1667
Jeremiah Taylor, 1667
William Harris, 1675
John Page, 1677 – 1687
Cope D'Oyley, 1687
James Wallace, 1691 – 1712

The Eighteenth Century

Andrew Thompson, 1712 – 1719
James Falconer, 1720 – 1724
Thomas Peador, 1727 – 1731
William Fyfe, 1731 – 1755
Thomas Warrington, 1756 – 1770
William Selden, 1771 – 1783

William Nixon, 1783 – 1784
William Bland, 1786 – 1787
Henry Skyren, 1787 – 1795
John Jones Spooner, 1796 – 1799
Benjamin Brown, 1799 – 1806

The Nineteenth Century

Robert Seymour Symms, 1806
George Holson, 1810 – 1813
Mark L. Chevers, 1827 – 1843
John F. Bausman, 1843 – 1844
William H. Goode, 1845 – 1848
John C. McCabe, 1850 – 1856
Edward H. Harlow, 1856 – 1858

William F. M. Jacobs, 1860 – 1861
John McCarty, 1869 – 1871
John J. Norwood, 1871 – 1872
William Jarrett, 1873 – 1875
J. W. Keeble, 1875 – 1876
John J. Gravatt, 1876 – 1893
C. Braxton Bryan, 1893 – 1905

The Twentieth Century

Reverdy Estill, 1905 – 1911
Edwin R. Carter, 1912 – 1922
Charles E. McAllister, 1922 – 1926
George O. Watts, 1927 – 1931

Theodore S. Will, 1932 – 1938
Carter H. Harrison, 1938 – 1959
Francis W. Hayes, Jr., 1960 – 1979
Rodney L Caulkins, 1980 – 1999

The Twenty-First Century

Keith N. Adams, 2001 – 2002
Donna-Mae Siderius, 2003 -

Appendix II
Ministers of Elizabeth City Parish buried at the church sites and Their Years of Ministry

At The Third Site (Pembroke):

James Wallace, 1691 – 1712
Andrew Thompson, 1712 -1719

At The Fourth Site:

Henry Skyren, 1787 – 1795
John Jones Spooner, 1796 – 1799
Benjamin Brown, 1799 – 1806
Mark L. Chevers, 1827 – 1843
John C. McCabe, 1850 – 1856
John J. Gravatt, 1876 – 1893
Reverdy Estill, 1905 – 1911
Edwin R. Carter, 1912 – 1922
George O. Watts, 1927 – 1931
Theodore S. Will, 1932 – 1938
Carter H. Harrison, 1938 - 1959

References Cited

Archuleta, Margaret L. et als, *Away from Home,* Phoenix, AR.: The Heard Museum, 2000

Argall, Samuel, *Letter to Hawes, June 1613,* Modern version in: *Jamestown Narratives Eyewitness Accounts of the Virginia Colony, The First Decade, 1607-1617*: Ed. Edward Wright Haile, Champlain, Va.: Roundhouse, 1998.

Bentley, John B., *Gravestone Inscriptions from the Cemetery of St. John's Episcopal Church, Hampton, Virginia,* Hampton, Va.: The Hugh S. Watson Genealogical Society of Tidewater Virginia, 1975.

Blackburn, Joyce, *George Wythe of Williamsburg,* New York: Harper and Row, 1975

Bond, Edward L. and Joan R. Gundersen, *The Episcopal Church in Virginia 1607-2007,* Richmond, Va.: Episcopal Diocese of Virginia, 2007.

Brittingham, Joseph B. and Alvin W. Sr., *The First Trading Post at Kicotan,* Newport News, Va.: Franklin Printing, 1947.

Brown, Alexander, *The First Republic in America,* Boston and New York: Houghton, Mifflin and Company, 1898.

_____, *The Genesis of America,* New York: Russell and Russell, 1964.

Brown, Chester, Religion's Special Role, *From the Sea to the Stars,* third edition, Virginia Beach, Va.: The Donning Company Publishers, 2004

Bruce, Philip A., *Social Life in Virginia in the Seventeenth Century*, Williamstown, Mass.: Corner House, 1968.

Brydon, George Maclaren, *Virginia's Mother Church*, Richmond, Va.: Virginia Historical Society, 1947.

Butler, H. Joseph, *The Peter Pelham Manuscript of 1744*, Colfax, N.C.: Wayne Leopold Editions, 2005.

Carr, Frances Dale, *The Daily Press*, Newport News, Va.: February 1, 1958.

Chase, Salmon P., *The Chase Papers*, Library of Congress.

Cleaveland, George J., *The Church of Virginia, Established and Dispossessed*, an article in *Up From Independence*, Orange, Va.: Green Publishers, Inc., 1976.

Council of Virginia, *A True Declaration of the estate of the colony in Virginia...,1610*. Modern version in *Jamestown Narratives, Eyewitness Accounts of the Virginia Colony, the First Decade: 1607-1617*, Ed. Edward Wright Haile, Champlain, Va.: Roundhouse, 1998.

Dale, Thomas, *Letter to the Council of Virginia*, 25 May 1611. Modern version in *Jamestown Narratives, Eyewitness Accounts of the Virginia Colony, The First Decade: 1607-1617*, Ed. Edward Wright Haile, Champlain, Va.: Roundhouse, 1998.

The Daily Press, Newport News, Va.

Eckenrode, H. J., *The Revolution in Virginia*, New York: Houghton Miflin Co, 1916.

Engs, Robert F., *Freedom's First Generation*, New York: Fordham University Press, 2004.

Evans, Dandridge, *Lost Landmarks of Old Hampton. Revolutionary War Port Town*, Hampton: Hampton Association for the Arts and Humanities, 1976.

Fleming, G. James., *The Norfolk Journal and Guide*: October 10, 1931.

George, Chrisopher T., *Terror on the Chesapeake*, Shippensburg, Pa.: White Mane Books, 2000.

Gundry Beverly F. Gundry, *Fort Monroe Historical Society Newsletter*, July, 1982.

Haile, Edward Wright, Ed. *Jamestown Narratives, Eyewitness Accounts of the Virginia Colony, the First Decade: 1607-1617,* Ed. Edward Wright Haile, Champlain, Va.: Roundhouse, 1998.

Hall, Cornelius Cornick, Jr., *Portraits in the Collection of the Virginia Historical Society,* Charlottesville, Va.: University Press of Virginia, 1981.

Hamor, Ralph, *A True Discourse of the present estate of Virginia.* Modern version in *Jamestown Narratives, Eyewitness Accounts of the Virginia Colony, the First Decade: 1607-1617,* Ed. Edward Wright Haile, Champlain, Va.: Roundhouse, 1998.

Hayes, Francis W., Jr., *Report to the Vestry of St. John's Church,* Hampton Va., 1981.

Heffelfinger, Jacob, *Kecoughtan Old and New or Three Hundred Years of Elizabeth City Parish,* Hampton, Va.: Houston Publishing and Printing,1910.

Heffelfinger, *Heffelfinger Diaries,* Hampton History Museum, Hampton, Va. 1861-1865.

Hening, William W., *Statues at Large from the First Session of the Legislature in 1619, Volume I,* New York: R.W. & G. Bartow, 1823.

Higgins, Thomas F. III and Charles M. Downing, *Phase III Archeological Investigations At the Tysinger and Carousel Plaza/Park Blocks, City of Hampton, Virginia,* Williamsburg, Va.: The College of William and Mary, 1993.

Hodges, George, *Three Hundred Years of the Episcopal Church in America,* Philadelphia, Pa.: George W. Jacobs & Co., 1906.

Holt, Eleanor, *The Second Church of Elizabeth City Parish 1623/4-1698,* Richmond, Va.: Archeological Society of Virginia, 1985.

Holmes David L., *The Decline and Revival of the Church of Virginia,* an article in *Up From Independence,* Orange, Va.: Green Publishers, Inc. 1976.

Horn, James, *A Land as God Made It, Jamestown and the Birth of America,* New York: Basic Books, 2005.

Jensen, Les, *32nd Virginia Infantry,* Lynchburg, Va.: H.E. Howard, Inc., 1990.

Lombardi, Michael, *Colonial Williamsburg,* Williamsburg, Va: Colonial Williamsburg, Aurumn 2007.

Mason, George C., *Colonial Churches of Tidewater Virginia,* Richmond, Va.: Whittet and Shepperson, 1945.

McCabe, John B. *Glover's Colonial Churches in Virginia: St. John Church, Hampton, International Magazine,* January 1852.

_____, *Address Delivered before the Patrons and Pupils of Hampton Academy, July 30, 1853,* Richmond, Va.: 1853.

Meade, William, *Old Churches Ministers and Families of Virginia,* Philadelphia: Genealogical Publishing Co., Inc., 1857.

Montague, E. Sclater, #20, Syms Eaton Museum Horn Book Series, Hampton, Va.

_____, *A Hodgepodge of Memories of Hampton,* Hampton, Va.: Houston Printing, 1972

Morton, Richard L., *Colonial Virginia,* Chapel Hill, N.C.: The University of North Carolina Press, 1960.

Neal, Rosemary C. *Elizabeth City County, Virginia, Deeds, Wills, Court Orders, Etc. 1634,1659, 1699-1702.*Hampton, Va.: Port Hampton Press, 2007.

____, *Elizabeth City County, Virginia, Deeds, Wills, Court Orders, 1715-1721,* Hampton Va.: Port Hampton Press, 2007.

Osborne, William H., *The History of the Twenty-Ninth Regiment of Massachusetts Volunteer Infantry in the Late War of the Rebellion,* Boston, Albert J. Wright, 1877.

Percy, George, *Observations gathered out of a discourse of the plantation of the colony in Virginia by the English, 1606.* Modern version in *Jamestown Narratives, Eyewitness Accounts of the Virginia Colony, the First Decade, 1607-1617,* Ed. Edward Wright Haile, Champlain, Va.: Roundhouse, 1998.

_____, *A True Relation of the proceedings and occurrences that have hap'ned in Virginia from the time Sir Thomas Gates was shipwrack'd upon the Bermudes, Anno 1609, until my departure out of the country, which was in anno Domini 1612.* Modern version in *Jamestown Narratives, Eyewitness Accounts of the Virginia Colony, the First Decade: 1607-1617,* Ed Edward Wright Haile, Champlain, Va.: Roundhouse. 1998.

Quarstein, John V. *The Civil War on the Virginia Peninsula,* Dover N.H.: Arcadia Publishing, 1997.

_____, John V. and Dennis Mroczkowski, *Fort Monroe, the Key to the South,* Charleston, S.C.: Arcadia Publishing, 2000.

Raper, Derris L. and Jones, Constance M., *A Goodly Heritage, The Episcopal Diocese of Southern Virginia 1892-1992, Norfolk, Va.*: Pictorial Heritage Publishing Company, 1992.

Rolfe, John, *A True Relation on the State of Virginia.* Modern version in *Jamestown Narratives, Eyewitness Accounts of the Virginia Colony, the First Decade: 1607 1617,* Ed. Edward Wright Haile, Champlain, Va.: Roundhouse, 1998.

Rountree, Helen, *Pocahontas, Opechancanough, and Powhatan, Three Indian Lives Changed by Jamestown,* Charlottesville Va.: University of Virginia Press, 2005.

St. Cyprian's Church, A Brief History, Archives of St. Cyprian's Church

St. John's Church Vestry Book, St. John's Church, Hampton, Va. 1910,2002, 2003

Schlegel, Marvin W. *The Shire of Elizabeth City County, 1634-1700,* from *History of Lower Tidewater Virginia,* Ed. Rogers D. Whichard, New York: Lewis Historical Publishing Company, 1959.

_____, *Elizabeth City County and the Town of Hampton 1700-1814,* from *History of Lower Tidewater Virginia,* Ed. Rogers D. Whichard, New York: Lewis Historical Publishing Company, 1959.

Seiler, William H., *The Anglican Parish in Virginia,* Ed. James M. Smith, *Seventeenth=Century America,* Chapel Hill, N.C.: University of North Carolina Press, 1959.

Selden, Jefferson S., Jr., *Samuel Selden the Immigrant and his Wife Rebecca Yeo Selden,* Hampton, Va.: Jefferson S. Selden, Jr., 1980.

Selden, William, Memorandum book, 1779-1782, Manuscripts Department of the University of Virginia Library.

Smith, John, *The General History: The Third Book.* Modern version in *Jamestown Narratives, Eyewitness Accounts of the Virginia Colony, The First Decade:1607- 1617,* Ed. Edward Wright Haile, Champlain, Va.: Roundhouse, 1998.

Sneden, Robert K. *Eye of the Storm,* New York: The Free Press, 2000.

Strachey, William, *A True Reportory of the Wrack and Redemption of Sir Thomas Gates, Knight, upon and from the islands of the Bermudas; his coming to Virginia, and the Estate of that colony then, and after under the government of Lord La Warre, July 15, 1610.* Modern version in *Jamestown Narratives, Eyewitness Accounts of the Virginia Colony, the First Decade: 1607-1617,* Ed. Edward Wright Haile, Champlain, Va.: Roundhouse, 1998.

The Times Herald, Newport News, Va.

Tyler, Lyon G., *History of Hampton and Elizabeth City County, Virginia,* Hampton, Va.: Elizabeth City County, 1922.

VonDoenhoff, Marian Ruth, *The Vestry Book of Elizabeth City County,* a thesis for the College of William and Mary, March 1957.

vonSchilling, Jean Marshall, *Booker Descendants of Captain Richard Booker of Abingdon Parish, Gloucester County, Virginia,*1997.

West, George Ben, *When the Yankees Came,* Edited by Parke Rouse, Jr., Richmond, Va.: The Dietz Press, 1977.

Whichard, Rogers D. *History of Lower Tidewater Virginia,* New York: Lewis Historical Publishing Company, 1959.

Whitaker, Alexander, *Good News from Virginia.* Modern version in *Jamestown Narratives, Eyewitness Accounts of the Virginia Colony, the First Decade:1607-1617,* Ed. Edward Wright Haile, Champlain, Va.: Roundhouse,1998.

Will, Theodore S., *The Episcopal Church,* Milwaukee, Wis.: Morehouse Publishing Co., 1934.

Williamson, Gene, *Of the Sea and Skies, Historic Hampton and its Times,* Bowie, Md.: Heritage Books, 1993.

_____, *Chesapeake Conflict, the Troublesome Early Days of Maryland,* Bowie, Md.: Heritage Books, 1995.

Wise, Kate Ellis, *The Wise Guide to Historic Places in Virginia,* Hampton, Va.: Virginia Printing and Publishing Company, 1907

Endnotes

Chapter One — A Place Called Kecoughtan
1. The charter of the Virginia Company, Haile, 1998: 15
2. Rev. Hunt's sickness and perseverance, Smith, Haile, 1998: 223
3. The landing at Kecoughtan, Percy, *Observations ,* Haile 1998: 91
4. Christmas at Kecoughtan, 1608, Smith, Haile, 1998: 297
5. Thomas Gates' attack on Kecoughtan, Strachey, Haile, 1998: 435
6. Powhatan's attack on Kecoughtan, Rountree, 2005: 27
7. "inhabitants of a great town," *Of the Sea and Skies*, Williamson, 1993: 22

Chapter Two — The First Church, 1610
1. Archeology at Kecoughtan trading post, Brittingham, 1947: 10
2. Fort at Kecoughtan, Percy, *A True Relation;* Haile,1998: 508-509
3. Planting at Kecoughtan, Dale, Haile, 1998: 522.
4. Examination on faith by minister, Brydon, 1947: 18
5. Whitaker's description of Indians, Whitaker, Haile, 1998: 731
6. Release of William Parker, Hamor, Haile, 1998: 835-836
7. Rolfe's Report to King James, Rolfe, Haile, 1998: 874
8. Political subdivisions in 1619, Brydon, 1947: 35-37
9. The Reverend Keith's appointment, Brydon, 1947: 49

Chapter Three — A Place of Refuge
1. The Reverend Keith's tenure. Brydon, 1947: 42
2. Establishment of Martin's and Smith's Hundreds: Brydon, 1947: 34
3. Gift of Mrs. Mary Robinson, Brydon, 1947: 56
4. Description of The Reverend White, Brydon, 1947: 421

5. Mortality in 1620, Brown, 1898: 415
6. Hospital at Hampton, Heffelfinger, 1910: 10
7. Daniel Gookin at "New Porte Newce", Brown, 1898: 459
8. Death of Rev. Keith in Massacre of 1622, Whichard, 1959:71
9. Elizabeth City Muster of 1623, Heffelfinger, 1910: Appendix B
10. Escape of Edward Waters to Elizabeth City, Brown, 1898: 473
11. William Capps on the effect of the Great Massacre of 1622, Horn, 2005: 261

Chapter Four — *The Second Church, 1624*
1. Description of church at second site, Holt, 1985: 78,84
2. Amount and method of paying workmen's wages, Holt, 1985: 74
3. Adventures of Edward Waters, Brown, 1964: 1042-1043
4. Death of the Rev. White, Brydon, 1947: 42
5. Appointment of The Rev. Stockton, Holt, 1985: 10
6. The communion silver of St. John's Church, Holt, 1985: 13-15

Chapter Five — *Church and State*
1. Legacy of Sir Edwin Sandys, Brydon, 1947: 71
2. Role of the government in the absence of bishops, Brydon, 1947: 67
3. Acts of the General Assembly, 1623-1624, Hening, 1823: 122-124
4. Controversy between The Rev. Graeme and Captain Tucker, Holt, 1985: 17
5. Family and servants of Captain Tucker, Schlegel, *The Shire or County of Elizabeth City...,* 1959: 111
6. The beginnings of the vestry system, Brydon, 1947: 90-92
7. Benefit of Clergy requested by William Reade, Holt, 1985: 18

Chapter Six — *Parish Life*
1. Growth of Elizabeth City, Holt, 1985: 26
2. Appointment of The Rev. Wilkinson, Holt, 1985: 30
3. Place of church in the social life of colonists, Bruce, 1968: 239
4. Artifacts found at the second church, Holt, 1985: 98-138
5. Seventeenth century weddings and funerals, Bruce, 1968: 234-235, 219-222
6. Will of Daniel Hopkinson, Holt, 1985: 27
7. Attendance at cock fights, Wise, 1907: 41
8. Establishment of the Syms and Eaton schools, Starkey, 1967: 13
9. Duties of the vestry, Brydon, 1947: 94-95

Chapter Seven — Strife and the Great Storm

1. Administration and removal of Governor Sir John Harvey, Brydon, 1947: 114
2. Departure of three hundred Puritans for Maryland, Brydon, 1947: 119
3. Son of Daniel Gookin leaves Newport News for Boston, Starkey, 1967: 11
4. Altercation between The Reverend Alymer and Mr. Bushrod, Holt, 1985: 51
5. Land patent of The Reverend Alymer, Holt, 1985: 38
6. William Claiborne's trading base in Elizabeth City, Williamson, *Chesapeake Conflict,* 1995: 9
7. Windmill built by William Claiborne, Schlegel, *The Shire or County of Elizabeth City...,* 1959: 113
8. The hurricane of 1667, Holt, 1985: 189-190
9. Number of men living near fort at Old Point Comfort in 1667, Neal, *Elizabeth City County, Virginia...1634...1986:* xi
10. Permission to move church to Pembroke Plantation, Williamson, *Chesapeake Conflict,* 1996:99

Chapter Eight — The Third Church, 1667

1. Burials at the second church, Holt, 1985: 84
2. Misbehavior of the Reverend Jeremiah Taylor, Schlegel, *The Shire or County of Elizabeth City...,*1959: 121
3. Rev. Taylor's behavior and the need for a bishop, Meade, 1857: 231, 15
4. Acts of General Assembly in 1662, Hening, 1823, Vol II: 44-51
5. Apprenticeship court order of Robert Cradocke, Neal, *Elizabeth City County, Virginia...1634...1986:* 86
6. Freedom of Abraham Saby from County taxes, Neal, *Elizabeth City County, Virginia...1634...* 1986: 104
7. Remarriage of Elizabeth Bacon, Schlegel, *The Shire or County of Elizabeth City...,*1959: 128
8. Court appearances of the Reverend Wallace, Heffelfinger, *Kecoughtan Old and New,* 1910:19
9. Court appearances for non-attendance at church, Neal, *Elizabeth City County..., 1715...,*1986: 75-77
10. Service of the Reverend Andrew Thompson, Heffelfinger, *Kecoughtan Old and New,* 1910: 20-21

Chapter Nine — Port Hampton

1. References to Thomas Curle, "gentleman", in court records, Neal, *Elizabeth City County, Virginia…1634…,1986:* see index
2. Peter Heyman's death in battle with pirates, Schlegel, 1959: 131-132
3. Importance of Hampton as a port, Williamson, *Of the Sea and Skies, 1993: 121*
4. Growth of the port of Hampton, Neal, *Elizabeth City County, Virginia…1715…*, 1986: ix-x

Chapter Ten — The Fourth Church, 1728

1. Report of the Reverend Falconer, Heffelfinger, *Kecoughtan Old and New,* 1910: 21
2. Effects of the Religious Toleration Act, Schlegel, *Elizabeth City County…*, 1959: 144-145
3. Construction of the fourth church, Mason, 1945: 108-109
4. Interior details of the fourth church, Heffelfinger, *Kecoughtan Old and New,* 1910: 21-22
5. Organist Peter Pelham in Hampton, Butler, 2005: 8-9.12
6. Stability of ministerial appointments in Virginia, Brydon, 1947: 376-377
7. Description of the Reverend Fyfe, Schlegel, *Elizabeth City County…*, 1959:146
8. Description of Sunday morning at the fourth church, Heffelfinger, *Kecoughtan Old and New,* 1910: 25
9. Wilson Miles Cary, collector of custom in 1769, Tyler,1922: 36

Chapter Eleven — The Approaching Conflict

1. Removal of wooden chimneys, Starkey, 1967: 43
2. Population of Hampton and Elizabeth City County, Tyler,1922: 36, 39
3. Hurricane damage in 1749, Williamson, *Of the Sea and Skies,* 1993: 135
4. Growth of other denominations, Cleaveland, 1976: 39-40
5. Parish expenditures, 1751, vonDoenhoff, 1957: 10-14
6. Vestry provision for the sick and the poor, vonDoenhoff, 1957: xxiii-xxiv
7. Improvements to the fourth church, Schlegel, *Elizabeth City County…*, 1959: 146-147
8. Appointment of William Selden to the church, Heffelfinger, *Kecoughtan Old and New,* 1910: 22, 25-26
9. Thomas Wythe III a vestryman of the church at Hampton, Blackburn, 1975: 3
10. Prominence of George Wythe, Starkey, 1967: 44

11. Celebration in the taverns at Hampton, Higgins and Downing, 1993: 43
12. The Battle of Hampton, Starkey, 1967: 46-47
13. Royal insignia struck by lightning, Tyler, 1922: 40

Chapter Twelve — The Revolution

1. Arguments of George Wythe, *Of the Sea and Skies,* Williamson, 1993: 146
2. Hampton and the Virginia Navy, *Of the Sea and Skies,* Williamson, 1993: 147
3. Production of salt for the war, *Of the Sea and Skies,* Williamson, 1993: 148
4. Lookouts at Point Comfort, Starkey, 1967: 46
5. Income of Rev. Seldon from private pupils. Seldon Memo. Book,1779-1782
6. The Barron family in the Revolution, Tyler, 1922:42
7. James Barron captures a troop ship, Eckenrode, 1916: 94
8. Death of Colonel Francis Mallory, Schlegel, *Elizabeth City County...,* *1959*: 159
9. Presentation of prayer Book to Rev. Selden, *Samuel Seldon the Immigrant and his Wife Rebecca Yeo Seldon,* 1980:7
10. Decline of Hampton as a port, Starkey, 1967: 49

Chapter Thirteen — The Church in Transition

1. Rev. Selden's retirement and successor, Heffelfinger, *Kecoughtan Old and New,*1910: 27-28
2. Employment of the Rev. Nixon, Schlegel, *Elizabeth City County...,* 1959: 161
3. Actions of the General Assembly and Overseers of the Poor, Heffelfinger, *Kecoughtan Old and New,*1910: 28
4. Inpact of seizure of the glebes, Holmes, 1975: 58
5. Condition of the church yard in 1788, Schlegel, *Elizabeth City County...,*1959: 161
6. Removal of the bell from the tower, Mason, 1857: 236
7. Consecration of the Bishop of Virginia, Hodges.1906: 90-94
8. Service of James Madison as Bishop of Virginia, Holmes, 1976: 64-67
9. Ministers at Hampton 1786 through 1806, Heffelfinger, *Kecoughtan Old and New,* 1910: 28-29
10. Rachel Garrett's marriage to Count Rochambeau, Schlegel, *Elizabeth City County...,*1959: 161
11. Vacancies in the pulpit at Hampton, Schlegel, *Elizabeth City County...,* 1959: 162

Chapter Fourteen — The War of 1812

1. Establishment of Hampton Academy, Schlegel, *Elizabeth City County...*, 1959: 164
2. Achievements of Commodore Warrington, Tyler, 1922: 45-46
3. British targets in Chesapeake Bay, George, 2000: 40
4. Conduct of British after Battle of Hampton, George, 2000: 51
5. Precipitous British departure from Hampton, Starkey, 1967: 56
6. Looting at Hampton, Schlegel, *Elizabeth City County...*,1959: 166
7. Compensation for war damages, Schlegel, *Elizabeth City County...*, 1959: 167
8. Damage to church at Hampton, Mason, 1945: 113

Chapter Fifteen — The Restoration

1. "If I were a man..." Meade, 1857: 237
2. Consecration of Bishop Moore, Bond, 2007: 63
3. Words of Bishop Moore on restoration, Heffelfinger, *Kecoughtan Old and New,* 1910: 31-32
4. Subscription to restore the church, Heffelfinger, *Kecoughtan Old and New,* 1910: 31
5. Details of restored church, Mason, 1945: 114
6. Ministry of Mark Chevers, Gundry, 1982:1-3

Chapter Sixteen — A Pretty Little Town

1. Strengthening the church, Bond and Gundersen, 2007: 65
2. Diocesean position on low church and slavery, Bond and Gundersen, 2007: 94-101
3. Visit of Bishop Johns. Heffelfinger, 1910: 34
4. Ministry of the Reverends Bausman and Goode, Heffelfinger, *Kecoughtan Old and New,* 1910: 34
5. Letter from Edgar Allan Poe to the Reverend McCabe, Poe Collection, University of Virginia Library, 1836
6. Discovery of the third site of the church at Hampton, McCabe, 1852: 42
7. Antebellum amenities available on the Virginia Peninsula, Williamson, *Of the Sea and Skies,*1993: 175
8. Excerpt from the Reverend McCabe's address at Hampton Academy, McCabe, 1853
9. Other churches in Hampton, Brown, 2004: 71-74
10. Description of the lost town, Starkey, 1967: 74-76

Chapter Seventeen — *The Burning of Hampton*
1. Reinforcement of Fort Monroe, Quarstein and Mroczkowski, 2000: 30-32
2. "The war came just as suddenly as a flash of lightning," Starkey, 1967: 77
3. Closing the polls in Hampton, Jensen, 1990: 16
4. Evacuation of Hampton, Heffelfinger, *Kecoughtan Old and New,* 1910: 35
5. Appearance of Hampton, May 1861, Jensen, 1990: 19
6. Withdrawal of Federal troops from Hampton after the first battle of Manassas, Quarstein, 1997: 51
7. "the flaming torches were seen dancing," Osborne, 1877: 79
8. "a more desolate sight cannot be imagined," Quarstein, 1997: 55
9. "The fire had gutted it completely." Sneden, 2000: 30-31
10. Lincoln's visit to Hampton. Chase, Vol. III, Correspondence, pps 189-190

Chapter Eighteen — *The Civil War*
1. Departure of the Reverend Jacobs, Heffelfinger, *Kecoughtan Old and New,* 1910: 35
2. Robert Sneden's observations, Sneden, 2000: 33
3. Migration of escaped slaves to lower Virginia Peninsula, Engs, 2004: 27
4. Activities of freedmen, Engs, 2004: 20-24
5. Service of George Booker, vonSchilling, 1997: 110-112
6. 2nd capture of Jacob Heffelfinger, *Heffelfinger Diary, 1862*: 12/13/62-12/31/62
7. Service of Dr. George W. Semple, Jensen, 1990: 201
8. Return of George Ben West to Hampton, West, 1977: 99

Chapter Nineteen — *Rebuilding Again*
1. Plight of returning Peninsula residents, West, 1977: 100
2. St. John's temporary arrangements and restoration, Heffelfinger, 1910: 36
3. Heffelfinger's Civil War visit to St. John's Church, Heffelfinger, 1910: 40
4. Postwar economic activity at Hampton, *Of the Sea and Skies,* Williamson, 1993: 201-202
5. Arrival of the Reverend Gravatt, Montague, #20, Syms Eaton Museum Hornbook Series
6. Growth during ministry of John Gravatt, Heffelfinger, 1910: 38-39

Chapter Twenty — *A Time of Mission*
1. Creation of Diocese of Southern Virginia, Bond and Gundersen, 2007: 120
2. Beginnings of Emmanuel Church, Phoebus, Carr, 1958: 3D
3. Service of the Reverend Gravatt, Montague, #20, Syms Eaton Museum Horn Book Series

4. Personality of the Reverend Bryan, Montague, #20, Syms Eaton Museum Horn Book Series
5. Gratitude of E. Sclater Montague, Montague, #20, Syms Eaton Museum Horn Book Series
6. Sunday school for black students, Journal of the Diocese of Southern Virginia, 1904: 137
7. Beginning of St. Cyprian's Church, *"A Brief History of St. Cyprian's Church"*
8. Mrs. Virginia Tabb's gift of the second church site to St. John's Church, Holt, 1985: 203-204
9. Funeral services for the Reverend Reverdy Estill, *The Times Herald,* May 24-26, 1911

Chapter Twenty-One — *Make a Joyful Noise*
1. Choir of Indian students, Archuleta, 2000: 83
2. Musical talent of the Reverend Carter, Montague, #20, Syms Eaton Musuem Horn Book Series
3. Enlargement of the parish house, Vestry Book, April, 1910
4. Mobilization of Battery D, Montague, 1972: *A Hodgepodge of Memories Of Hampton,*: 48
5. Service of the Reverend McAllister, Montague, #20, Syms Eaton Museum Horn Book Series
6. Service of the Reverend Watts, Montague, #20, Syms Eaton Museum Horn Book Series
7. ECW leadership of Mollie Darling, Raper and Jones, 1922: 136-137
8. Montague's memory of Mollie Darling, Montague, 1972: 45

Chapter Twenty-Two — *Swing Low, Sweet Chariot*
1. The Reverend Will's book, Will, 1934
2. Loss of vestry support for the Reverend Will, Montague, #20, Syms Eaton Museum Horn Book Series
3. John Bentley's transcription of the Frenchman's map, Lombardi, 2007: 24
4. John Bentley's service to the Diocese of Southern Virginia, Raper and Jones, 1992: 109
5. Gravestone Inscriptions, St. John's Church Cemetery, Bentley, 1975
6. Solomon Fosque's knowledge of the St. John's cemetery, *The Norfolk Journal And Guide,* October 10, 1931
7. Funeral of Solomon Fosque, *The Daily Press,* March 8, 1936
8. The Balfours of "Little England", Hall, 1981: 20
9. Description of the cemetery, *St. John's Episcopal Church Cemetery, Hampton, Va,* Gregg Bleam Landscape Architects, 1999

Chapter Twenty-Three — To Be a Light
1. Organist and choirmaster Harold Chapman, *The Daily Press*, July 8, 1974
2. Mission church of St. Mark's, Raper and Jones, 1922: 200-201
3. Archeological exploration of second site, Holt, 1985
4. The Reverend Hayes call to recommitment, Hayes, 1970: 2-7

Chapter Twenty-Four — Feed My Sheep
1. Resignation of the Reverend Keith Adams, Vestry Book, May 14, 2002
2. Installation of the Very Reverend Donna-Mae Siderius, Vestry Book January, 2003
3. Number of communicants in 2008. St. John's Church Records

Illustrations

Acknowledgements

I would like to acknowledge first the efforts of Beverly Gundry, the historian of St. John's Church, to conserve documents and images from the church's history. William Boyer of St. John's staff was most helpful in making these resources accessible to me.

Besides the Very Reverend Donna Mae Siderius and the St. John's church staff, I am grateful to members of the community who have been of assistance. In particular, I wish to acknowledge assistance from the staff of the Virginiana Room of the Hampton Library. Likewise, I am indebted to the staff of the Virginiana Room of the Main Street Library of Newport News. Curator Michael Cobb of the Hampton History Museum provided useful information on the church at the second site. The City of Hampton's Information Technology staff created the three maps used in the book. The library of the Virginia Historical Society in Richmond and the Rockefeller Library in Williamsburg were also sources of information. The staffs of St. Paul's Church in Newport News, Emmanuel Church in Hampton, and St. Cyprian's Church in Hampton helped in understanding the relationship of their churches to St. John's Church. Hampton Historian John V. Quarstein reviewed the book and made many helpful suggestions.

I am especially grateful to Shannon McCall who used her artistic talent to illustrate the four church sites with a technique that evokes a sense of antiquity. I am also indebted to Robert Harper for his photographs.

Some of the prominent figures in St. John's history have also played a part in the preservation of that history. Jacob Heffelfinger, who recalled visiting the ruins of the church while recovering from his Civil War wounds, produced a history of the church along with his many other services to the people of St. John's. The Reverend Reverdy Estill, prominent in the period of church mission, also left an historical account.

I am indebted to my wife, Ann Darling Tormey, a lifelong member of St. John's Church, for many helpful suggestions in the preparation of this book and for her careful review of the manuscript.

Index